Jesus & The Land

Charles R. Page II

ABINGDON PRESS
Nashville

JESUS AND THE LAND

Copyright © 1995 by Abingdon Press

This book is printed on acid-free paper.

Library of Congress Cataloging-in-Publication Data

Page, Charles R.
  Jesus and the land / Charles R. Page II.
    p. cm.
  Includes bibliographical references (p.   ) and index.
  ISBN 0-687-00544-2 (alk. paper)
  1. Jesus Christ—Person and Offices.   2. Bible.N.T. Gospels—Geography.   3. Bible. N.T. Gospels—History of Biblical events.   4. Bible. N.t. Gospels—History of contemporary events.   5. Palestine—Social life and customs—To 70 A.D.   I. Title.
BT301.2.P34   1995
226'.091—dc20   95-7415
                                                                                                                 CIP

ISBN 13: 978-0-687-00544-4

06 07 08 09 10 11 12 13 14 15—10 9

MANUFACTURED IN THE UNITED STATES OF AMERICA

To my partner, soulmate, best friend,
love of my life, and devoted wife,
Judy Halfacre Page

CONTENTS

LIST OF ILLUSTRATIONS

10

FOREWORD

Shortly after earning my last degree, I returned to Israel where I met my colleague, friend, and spiritual mentor in Israel, Father Bargil Pixner. He took me to Capernaum and said he wanted to "see what I had learned." We entered the Franciscan park where people come to see the ruins of St. Peter's house and the fourth-century CE synagogue, and Bargil said, "So, tell me what you see!" I proceeded to talk about lintels, inscriptions, the insulaea, and the synagogue. He listened patiently. When I finished talking, he said, "Look deeper and tell me what you see." I explained to him about the millstones, olive presses, harbor, and the street running alongside the synagogue to the lake. He asked again, "What else?" I said, "That's about all I see."

He led me into the synagogue, and we sat on the bench that surrounds the interior wall. I could tell that he was disappointed, but I did not know why. He turned to me and said, "You must see Jesus here. If you do not see Jesus in the ruins of Capernaum, you should have studied physics. We are involved in biblical archaeology. Our job is to know him and to make him known. Seeing him helps us to know him. Knowing him leads us to love him. Loving him will help us to serve him and to make a difference in the world." Needless to say, it was a powerful experience for me. Sadly, I do not have the depth of faith as my brother, and too much of my own work and thought are centered in the mind and not the heart. But his comments were, nevertheless, right on target.

It is important to see and to know Jesus—not the Jesus of mythology, created by Western Protestant folk religion, but the historical Jesus who lived at a particular place in a specific time. Perhaps another story might illustrate this further. There was once an encounter between an older woman from a very conservative background and a more liberal, youthful male student pastor. The woman asked the young pastor, "Why couldn't the disciples stay awake in the Garden of Gethsemane the night Jesus was arrested?" The student pastor replied, "They were all probably drunk!" The elderly woman looked at the young pastor and said, "Baptists don't drink!" The pastor replied, "The disciples were Jewish." The woman replied again, "John the Baptist was the founder of the Baptist Church. He baptized Jesus, and Jesus became a Baptist, and so did the disciples—and Baptists don't drink!"

Certainly, Jesus was not a Baptist and neither were his associates. He was, indeed, Jewish and the product of both Jewish culture and first-century Middle Eastern peasant culture. Both of these aspects of his heritage supply us with insights into his life. Today, more than at any other time since these events were recorded, we have the opportunity to see Jesus through the eyes of archaeology, anthropology, and rabbinic and historical studies. The portrait of the Jesus of history that emerges is much different from the one we have created in Western folk religion. If Jesus is to matter at all, we must see and know him as he was. If his message is to have relevance in a complex technological age, we must hear this message clearly.

Recently there has been a resurgence in interest in the Jesus of history. This is appropriate, of course, because the historical Jesus has become lost in the Christ of faith. We cannot understand Jesus and his mission without an understanding of the times in which he lived. The purpose of *Jesus and the Land* is to attempt to recapture a sense of the historical Jesus based on recent discoveries and insights from the fields of archaeology, anthropology, Jewish history, historical geography, geology, and rabbinic studies. This book is an attempt to reconstruct a historical biography of the life of Jesus, and not an attempt to see Jesus through the eyes of nineteenth-century biblical criticism or biblical theology. The historian's question is not What do these stories mean? but rather What happened here, at this place and time?

At the risk of sounding heretical, for this work I have concluded that we must assume that some of the events reported in the New Testament are based on actual historic events. Certainly we must appreciate that the writers of the New Testament Gospels allowed their own theological hopes and beliefs to influence their reports. Nevertheless, we cannot summarily dismiss all of their work as mere theologized history. Too many events reported in the New Testament have historical antecedents in first-century peasant culture and Jewish religious Law. Jewish history, anthropology, rabbinic literature, and archaeology have validated many of the customs, practices, and examples found in the New Testament. For example, anthropological (and cultural) studies have demonstrated the importance of meals in the first (and twentieth) centuries. The New Testament also demonstrates the sacredness of sharing meals for various peoples. Rabbinic literature offers much insight into laws of purity and impurity in the formative years of Christian history. The New Testament also relates stories about people in the state of ritual uncleanness consistent with the rabbinic literature. Jewish history reports the ruthlessness of Herod and Pilate, also confirmed in the New Testament Gospels. The importance of the Gospels cannot be dismissed merely as biased reporting for the purpose of substantiating people's theological presuppositions. They stand on their own and must be taken seriously.

My previous work, *The Land and the Book: An Introduction to the World of the Bible*, coauthored with Carl A. Volz, mentioned the importance for the student of the Bible of having an understanding, a feel, if you will, for the Land of the Bible. The student of the Bible cannot fully understand or adequately interpret the writings of the Bible or the New Testament without coming to grips with the Land. In Israel, the Land is colloquially known as the "Fifth Gospel"! The same can be said for the life and teachings of Jesus. Without a knowledge, a sense of the Land, one is not able to adequately understand Jesus' work.

Jesus and the Land is an attempt to reconstruct the life of Jesus based on insights gained from the Land. How did Jesus' ministry begin? What led him from Nazareth and exclusive Judaism to Capernaum and inclusive Hillelian Judaism? What events led to the increase of his popularity, and how did this popularity result in his eventual execution? Our task is not easy; nor can it ever be complete. Too much information is unavailable. But it is possible to fill in pieces of the puzzle of Jesus' life by taking this interdisciplinary approach, by looking to the Land of the Bible as a background for our understanding of the historical Jesus. My goal in this work is to provide the reader an opportunity to see Jesus from the context of the Land. There are no great revelations here. This is the story of a man's life and times.

Chapter 1 provides the reader with a general historical overview. It is assumed that the reader has a working knowledge of the history of the Land, and perhaps this overview will serve as a refresher. Chapter 2 offers a prelude to ministry. Here we will look at customs related to childbirth, the rearing of children, the birth narratives, and events leading to the beginning of Jesus' ministry in Galilee. Chapter 3 is a look at Jesus' Galilean ministry, and chapter 4 is an analysis of the Judean ministry of Jesus.

I would like to acknowledge with gratitude those who have offered their assistance in the production of this new work. Rex D. Matthews, Senior Editor of Academic Books for Abingdon Press, has provided invaluable editorial assistance. Thank you for the support, criticism, advice, and encouragement. Also many thanks to Bob, Linda, and Steve for all of your hard work and support. I would also like to thank all of the students, past, present, and future, of the Jerusalem Center for Biblical Studies with whom I have dialogued over the years and who have traveled with me around the marvelous classroom of the Land of Israel. Special thanks go to my colleagues on the faculty (both full- and part-time) of the Jerusalem Center: Bargil Pixner, Lee Pattison, Pinhas Parot, Peter Miano, Dan Casey, Carl Volz, Barry Kiger, Chris Bullard, Ken Maahs, Gabriel Barkay, Isaiah Gaffnai, and Jimmy Namoor; and to our staff: Salim Lahham, our business manager in Jerusalem; Sevana Kharmandarian, our office manager at the Jerusalem Center; Kamel Bassa, who does so much for the students, faculty, and staff (behind the scenes); Ali Bolywon and his son Hussam; Barbara; Hani; Sahar; Eman; Hader; Mafouz; Eileen; and Daod. I wish to offer a special acknowledgment to Dr. James Ridgeway, the President of Educational Opportunities, and Dr. H. Chris Christiansen, Vice-President of Educational Opportunities, both of whom sit on the Board of Directors of the Jerusalem Center and both of whom have been dedicated friends to the students, staff, and faculty of the Jerusalem Center. I am also grateful to Kristine Haley, Dr. Sam Morris of the United Methodist Hour, and Bennet William (Bill) Bell for their helpful comments, questions, insights, and encouragement. Special thanks to Hugh Dean and Betty Fuller for your help.

Finally, I want to thank my family for their encouragement and support. My son, Jason, has served as a photographer for me. Many of the illustrations here are the result of his hard work, often hiking over long distances with camera in hand. His company traveling through the Land has been a special gift to me. He is not only my son but also one of my best friends. My parents, C. R. and Barbara Page, of Lick Creek, Tennessee, and my in-laws, Dearl and Joyce Halfacre of Chattanooga, Tennessee, have offered much-needed encouragement in the process. My daughters, Shannon amd Rebecca, special friends, who have always given me so much support. Thanks to Carol Adams and Sherry Aden for your love and encouragement. Most important, my wife, Judy Halfacre Page, has been my proofreader and has critiqued, questioned, corrected, affirmed, and supported the work and me from the outset of the project. Like Jason, she has spent long hours in the field, digging with me at Bethsaida and traveling through the Land as my partner, companion, and teacher. Without her patience and tolerance, as well as her assistance, this book could not have been written.

Charles R. Page II
Jerusalem Center for Biblical Studies
Jerusalem, Israel

CHAPTER ONE

THE LAND AND JESUS

Historical Overview

The Jewish people (Israelites or Hebrews) first settled in the Land during the migration from Egypt, usually associated with the exodus. The Galilee, according to Jewish history, was settled by four tribes: Asher, Issachar, Naphtali, and Zebulun. Yohanan Aharoni reports:

Asher, who took western Galilee, is already mentioned in Egyptian inscriptions from the end of the fourteenth century. They settled down as neighbours to the strong Phoenician coastal cities. . . . Issachar occupied the eastern part of the Jezreel Valley and the hills north of it. The tribe was consolidated mainly from among the corvée workers, part of whom had already come to this area during the Amarna period.

These two tribes [Issachar and Asher] belong to an early wave. They had penetrated into the well-developed Canaanite area in the north but were only able to gain a foothold there by remaining subservient to the powerful cities.

We do not know the circumstances surrounding the occupation by the other two tribes. The inheritance of Zebulun extended over the central part of southern Galilee between the Jezreel Valley and the Valley of Beth Netophah (Sahl el-Battof). Naphtali took a wide area in eastern and central Galilee. From the active participation of these two tribes in the war of Deborah it is permissible to conclude that at this date they were already well established in their areas.

An archaeological survey in Galilee proved that the Israelite settlement took place in the interior parts of Lower and Upper Galilee, which were forested and unoccupied during the Bronze

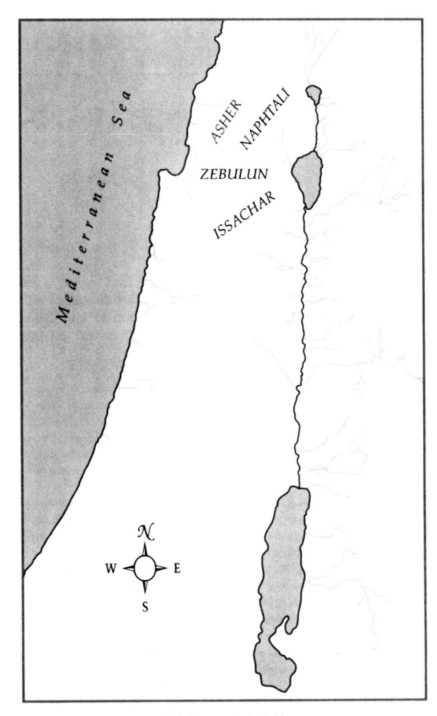

1. Tribal Territories in Galilee

Age. This is especially noticeable in the southern extremity of Upper Galilee which is the highest region of Galilee and the least convenient for settlement.[1]

By the Early Iron Age (12th and 11th centuries BCE) the majority of the Hebrew tribes had settled in the north (the regions of Samaria and Galilee). The tribes formed what has come to be called the Twelve Tribe Confederacy. The Bible reports a large gathering of the tribes at Shechem (Joshua 24), where the covenant is reaffirmed by Joshua and the people. This gathering at Shechem approximates the beginning of the Tribal Confederacy and the Period of the Judges. Little is known about the political association between the tribes at this time:

> Reconstruction of the precise political relationship among the Hebrew tribes during the period of the Judges is difficult. The older and once widely accepted interpretation was that Israel was organized into a religious confederacy called an amphictyony (comparable to the amphictyonies that existed among the Greeks). This view posited a considerable degree of organization among the tribes, based upon the existence of a central religious sanctuary to which each tribe sent representatives to observe an annual covenant renewal ceremony.
>
> Recent scholarship has challenged this view of Hebrew amphictyony, charging that it fails to deal with the ambiguity of the biblical evidence about the tribal interrelations or the inherent differences between the Hebrew and Greek societies. This does not mean that there was no cooperative alliance through which the Israelite tribes expressed their common allegiance to Yahwism or united in defensive actions. Rather, the Hebrew tribes were bound together in a loose confederacy that allowed the fullest possible autonomy to the separate tribes, but that also nurtured a common Israelite identity.[2]

In response to the growing Philistine threat, the tribes moved toward a common, centralized government. The first king was Saul (1020 BCE).[3] The Philistine threat was real; the fact that Philistine presence and dominance can be found as far north as Beth Shean indicates that they were a considerable force. Saul was killed in a battle with the Philistines at Mt. Gilboa in Lower Galilee. The Bible reports: "The next day, when the Philistines came to strip the dead, they found Saul and his three sons fallen on Mount Gilboa. They cut off his head, stripped off his armor, and sent messengers throughout the land of the Philistines to carry the good news to the houses of their idols and to the people. They put his armor in the temple of Astarte; and they fastened his body to the wall of Beth-shan" (1 Sam. 31:8-10).

For their mutual defense and protection, the northern tribes united with the southern tribes to form the United Monarchy under the rule of David (1000–961 BCE) and Solomon (961–922 BCE). This was a time of stability, peace, and prosperity. During this period the Philistine threat was neutralized and even other surrounding areas were subjugated to Israel.

The United Monarchy split into northern and southern kingdoms following the death of Solomon. Jeroboam I became the king of the northern tribes (in Israel), while Rehoboam I became the king of Judah in the south. As a part of the Northern Kingdom

2. *The Tel of Beth Shean. Saul's body was displayed on the walls of one of the cities built on this site.*

of Israel, Galilee fell under the domination of many surrounding powers for the next two centuries. Although the kings in the north sought to be strong and independent, only Omri and Ahab were able to establish a semblance of independence and power. In 733

BCE the Assyrians, under the leadership of Tiglath-Pileser III, received tribute from the citizens of the Northern Kingdom. Finally, after the king of Israel, Hoshea, withheld payment of this tribute and signed a defense treaty with Egypt, the Northern Kingdom finally fell to the Assyrians, who conquered their country, destroyed their capital city (Samaria), and deported many of the citizens in 722/721 BCE. Through this action by the Assyrians, the Northern Kingdom, in general, and Galilee, in particular, became a Gentile nation. For the first time since the conquest and settlement periods, we find a Jewish minority in the Galilee.

The prophet Isaiah refers to this era as a time of darkness in the land:

> But there will be no gloom for those who were in anguish. In the former time he brought into contempt the land of Zebulun and the land of Naphtali, but in the latter time he will make glorious the way of the sea, the land beyond the Jordan, Galilee of the nations.
>
> > The people who walked in darkness
> >   have seen a great light;
> > those who lived in a land of deep darkness—
> >   on them light has shined. (Isa. 9:1-2)

Darkness had come to the Galilee when the Gentiles drove the Jewish people from the land. Yet Isaiah says that one day the Jewish people will return to the north and to the Galilee, perhaps, when the Messiah comes.

For the next 130 years the Northern Kingdom was ruled by an outside power, while the Southern Kingdom (Judah) was ruled by the House of David. In 587/586 BCE, Judah fell to the Babylonians, and many of the Jewish people from Judah were exiled to Babylon. Unlike Israel in the north, many Jews remained in Judah during this exile, and foreigners were not imported into the country as they had been in the north. Judah remained a Jewish land. The situation and circumstances in the south are much different from those in the north. Through the exportation and importation policies of the Assyrians a new syncretic people came to dominate Galilee and the former Northern Kingdom. Even though many had been exiled to Babylon, the people of Judah retained their attachment to the Land by maintaining practices unique to their historical, ethnic, and religious heritage. For the people of Judah, self-understanding was intricately tied to this Land and to their religious, political, and cultural capital of Jerusalem.

In approximately 539 BCE the Persians conquered the Babylonians, and Cyrus, the Persian king, issued an official edict allowing the Jewish people to return to their homeland. Most of the Jews who had been living in exile in Babylon returned to Judah. They had been in exile for only some forty to fifty years and had maintained their bond with the Land. The same cannot be said, however, for the Jews who had been expelled from the Northern Kingdom. By this time the descendants of the northern tribes no longer had any bond with the land, and they, for the most part, chose not to return to their ancestral homeland. Thus the former Southern Kingdom maintained a Jewish majority, and the former Northern Kingdom retained a dominant Gentile majority. Galilee continued to be "Galilee of the nations [Gentiles]" (Isa. 9:1*b*).

The Greeks came to Palestine during the conquest of Alexander the Great. Alexander came to power following the death of his father, Philip II, in 336 BCE.[4] Shortly after becoming king, Alexander began his campaign to conquer Persia and lands farther to the east.

Our interest in Alexander's conquests is related to his seizing control of Palestine. Palestine was conquered as the result of two campaigns: the siege of Tyre, in ancient Phoenicia, and the siege of Gaza, which led to the conquest of Egypt. The siege of Tyre lasted seven months. Alexander was finally able to take the city by a combination of land and sea attacks. After the conquest of Tyre, he moved on to Egypt. Palestine fell under his control without any significant resistance. The city of Gaza was well fortified, and the Persian garrison there was able to resist for two months. After Gaza fell, however, there was little further resistance in Egypt. Of the surrender of Jerusalem, Carl Volz writes, "Josephus (*Antiquities* 11:329ff.) informs us that upon Alexander's arrival, the high priest went out to meet him with a large procession of dignitaries and offered his submission, together with a petition that the city be spared. Not only was the request granted, but Alexander also permitted the Jews to follow their traditional religious practices, both in Palestine and in Persia."[5]

Alexander died mysteriously in 323 BCE, thirteen years after he became king of Macedonia. He died without making provisions for a successor. Thus his kingdom was divided among his generals (known as the Diadochi, or Successors), some of whom went to war against one another immediately in territorial disputes. One general, Seleucus, became the king of Babylon, including Syria, in 321 BCE after the murder of Perdiccas. It took roughly thirteen years for Seleucus to consolidate his power there. A second general, Ptolemy I, was able to gain control in Egypt and Palestine by 306 BCE. Ptolemy made Alexandria his capital city. Because of the good relations that existed between the Jews and the Greeks as a result of Alexander's warm welcome in Jerusalem, many Jewish people migrated to Alexandria and comprised about 20 percent of the city's population. Furthermore, Ptolemy did not appoint a provincial governor to administer Palestine. Instead, he allowed the Jewish Council of Elders to continue to handle the administration of the land, under which the high priest exercised enormous power, functioning as a de facto governor.

There were several wars between the Seleucids and the Ptolemies over the next hundred years or so. The Seleucids were finally able to defeat the Ptolemies in a battle at Banyas (which would become Caesarea Philippi after the death of Herod the Great) in about 198 BCE to gain control of Palestine. Gradually their rule became more repressive, eventually leading to the Hasmonean or Maccabean Revolt. We must keep in mind that the Galilee was still dominated by Gentiles. The darkness spoken of by Isaiah was still present in Galilee—the Galilee of the Nations or the Galilee of the Gentiles.

Under Seleucid rule, life in Judea became more repressive. The Seleucid kings imposed a radical Hellenization plan on the Judeans. The people there, who had experienced religious tolerance and freedom under the Ptolemies, now found themselves being forced to adopt Greek customs and culture. In 190 BCE the Romans, the rising power from the west, were able to win several critical battles against the Seleucids. One of the major Roman victories occurred at Magnesia. As a result of this loss the Seleucids were forced to make outlandish financial payments to Rome. To help raise this money, the Seleucids imposed an oppressive tax against the citizens of Judea, Samaria, and Galilee. They also plundered the Temple treasury in Jerusalem, further alienating the citizens there. As another means of raising funds, the Seleucids instituted a new policy of auctioning the office of high priest to the highest bidder. The consequences of this policy were disastrous. The office changed often, and many of the men who assumed the office were hated by the masses, either for their own corruption or because they were not of the lineage of Aaron. Antiochus IV (Epiphanes) ascended to the throne of the Seleucid kingdom in 175 BCE. Since much of the former empire of Alexander to the west had been lost to the Romans, Antiochus IV conceived a plan to strengthen his kingdom to the east, perhaps establishing again a capital in Babylon. To this end, as reported in 1 Maccabees, he instituted a radical Hellenization plan on what was left of his kingdom, including Palestine and the Jewish people who lived there:

> Then the king [Antiochus] wrote to his whole kingdom that all should be one people, and that all should give up their particular customs. All the Gentiles accepted the command of the king. Many even from Israel gladly adopted his religion; they sacrificed to idols and profaned the sabbath. And the king sent letters by messengers to Jerusalem and the towns of Judah; he directed them to follow customs strange to the land, to forbid burnt offerings and sacrifices and drink offerings in the sanctuary, to profane sabbaths and festivals, to defile the sanctuary and the priests, to build altars and sacred precincts and shrines for idols, to sacrifice swine and other unclean animals, and to leave their sons uncircumcised. They were to make themselves abominable by everything unclean and profane, so that they would forget the law and change all the ordinances. He added, "And whoever does not obey the command of the king shall die." (1 Macc. 1:41-50)[6]

In short, Antiochus made it illegal to follow any practices or customs that were unique to the Jewish people under penalty of death. The final straw occurred in 167 BCE when Antiochus rededicated the Temple in Jerusalem to the Greek god Zeus and ordered the sacrifice of swine in the Holy of Holies. This was known as the "Abomination of Desolation."[7]

The Maccabean Revolt began when a reverent and holy priest named Mattathias refused to allow the sacrifice of a swine to Zeus in his home village of Modein (near modern-day Tel Aviv and Latrun) by killing a messenger who was sent with the orders to do so. Mattathias and his sons were forced to flee into the hill country of Judea, and there they began a guerrilla campaign against the Seleucids. Mattathias died in 166 BCE and leadership passed on to his son Judah (Judas). This small guerrilla band swept out of the hills and attacked the Greeks with such quickness and efficiency that they came to be known as the Maccabees, probably from the Hebrew word *maccabi*, which means "hammer." They hammered the Greeks with such skill that this small guerrilla army was able to force the Greeks to return to the policy of allowing the Jewish people to practice their religion in freedom.

The Greeks were finally driven out of certain sections of Jerusalem, and in 164 BCE the sons of Mattathias purified and rededicated the Temple.[8] Thus the goals of the revolt had been realized. The freedom to practice their faith had been restored. But during the revolt an emerging sense of nationalism was rekindled among the peasantry of Judea, and Judah and his brothers continued the struggle against the Greeks. Judah and his followers were able to win several battles against the Seleucids, but he was killed in a battle at Elasa in 160 BCE (see 1 Maccabees 9). Eventually his brothers and successors were able to defeat the Seleucids, which helped to solidify the power of the Maccabean (or Hasmonean[9]) family. Judah was succeeded by his brother Jonathan (161–143 BCE), who carried on the struggle. Finally, in 153 BCE, Jonathan was appointed high priest by the Syrian king Alexander, for Jonathan's support during a civil war in Syria.

Simon (143–135 BCE), the last surviving son of Mattathias, succeeded Jonathan, and he unified the various factions into a nation. He was able to drive the remaining Greeks out of Judea or to convert them to Judaism. About the rule of Simon, Menahem Stern writes:

> In 142 B.C.E. Simeon [Simon] had been granted the *de facto* status of an independent ruler, including the right to coin money

(which, however, he did not do) and an era of his own. The same rights were granted, or arrogated to themselves, by various Greek cities in Palestine and Phoenicia (Tyre in 125 B.C.E., Sidon in 111 B.C.E., Gaza and Ascalon before 103 B.C.E.). Local rulers, such as Zenon Cotylas in Philadelphia and Zoilus in Dora and the Tower of Straton, replaced the Seleucid officials. The Ituraeans occupied the slopes of Mt. Hermon and Lebanon, and gained a foothold on the Mediterranean; the Nabataeans extended their dominions as far as Damascus, the capital of Coele-Syria, under their king Aretas IV. In this free-for-all the Hasmonaeans took care to defend what they regarded as their 'patrimony,' the ancient kingdom of David. John Hyrcanus, Simeon's successor, gained a foothold on the king's highway east of the Jordan by taking Medaba and Samaga. (The other international highway through Palestine, the *via maris*, came under his dominion after the cession of Lydda). Hyrcanus then turned his attention to the Samaritans and Idumaeans. The conquest of Samaria was effected in two stages; first the Samaritan *ethnos* was subdued and their sanctuary on Mt. Gerizim ceased to function; nevertheless, the Samaritans kept their national and religious consciousness. Next the Idumaeans were conquered and converted to Judaism. From the beginning it had been the policy of the Hasmonaeans to tolerate no gentiles in their land; the conquered were asked to convert or to leave.[10]

As the Greeks moved out of Jerusalem, and eventually out of Judea to the north, they began slaughtering any Jewish people they might find, particularly in western Galilee. John Hyrcanus (135–105 BCE) organized his troops to rescue as many of the Jews who lived there as possible. For a brief period, there were no Jews living in most of Galilee. Hyrcanus was succeeded by his son, Judas Aristobulus, who ruled for only one year (104–103 BCE). Eventually, Alexander Jannaeus, a descendant of Judah, who ruled as king from 103–76 BCE, succeeded in driving the Gentiles out of Galilee. Thus around 100 BCE Jewish people returned to the Galilee and established the first Jewish population majority since the Assyrian conquest in 722/721 BCE. Jannaeus, although successful, was very unpopular with the general populace, and the people revolted against his rule (94–89 BCE).

Following the death of Jannaeus, his wife, Salome Alexandra, ruled for approximately nine years. Following her death in 69 BCE, a civil war broke out between the sons of Jannaeus and Salome Alexandra: Aristobulus II and John Hyrcanus II. The clash between these brothers eventually led to the Roman invasion under Pompey in 63 BCE. Pompey named Hyrcanus as ethnarch of Judea. After Julius Caesar defeated Pompey and gained control of the Roman army in the Eastern Province, Hyrcanus was appointed high priest and Herod the Great's father, Antipater, became procurator of Palestine. Antipater's sons were given powerful government positions. Phasael was appointed governor of Judea, and Herod became the governor in Galilee. Aristobulus was captured and taken to Rome where he and his family were later freed, a mistake on the part of the Romans. Shortly thereafter, Aristobulus's son Antigonus made a pact with the Parthians, the strong empire to the east in what is today Iran/Iraq. Antigonus agreed to make Palestine a vassal state of the Parthians if they would appoint him king and if the Parthians would help him to defeat Hyrcanus, Phasael, Herod, and the Romans. The invasion was successful, and Antigonus seized power in 40 BCE.

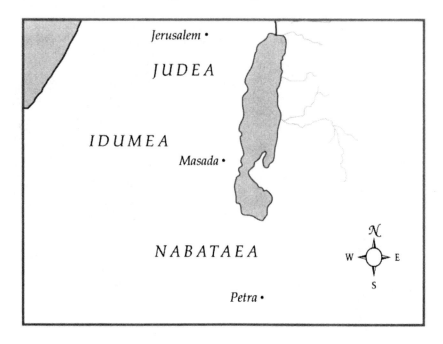

3. *Idumaea, Nabataea, Petra, Masada*

27

Herod the Great

Herod's grandfather Antipas had come to power in the service of Alexander Jannaeus as the governor of Idumea.[11] As noted above, after Julius Caesar defeated Pompey, Antipater (the son of Antipas and the father of Herod the Great) became procurator of Judea of Palestine. Antipater was assassinated in 43 BCE, which led to the instability that allowed Antigonus to plot to gain power in Palestine. After Antigonus successfully invaded and captured Judea and most of Jerusalem, Phasael and Herod were besieged in the family palace. Phasael and Hyrcanus decided to negotiate with Antigonus for their release. They were imprisoned, where Phasael died, either by execution or suicide, and where Hyrcanus's body was mutilated so that he could no longer serve in the position of high priest. About this Josephus writes: "And thus was Antigonus brought back into Judea by the king of the Parthians, and received Hyrcanus and Phasaelus for his prisoners . . . but being afraid that Hyrcanus, who was under the guard of the Parthians, might have

4. *The Fortress of Masada. Herod left his family here when he fled to Rome.*

his kingdom restored to him by the multitude, he cut off his ears, and thereby took care that the high priesthood should never come to him anymore, because he was maimed, while the law required this dignity should belong to none but such as had all their members entire" (*Antiquities* 14:365-366).

When Herod heard the news of the capture of Phasael and Hyrcanus, he fled with his family to Masada. There he left his family under the care of his younger brother Joseph. Josephus reports that Herod was accompanied by about nine thousand soldiers. When he and Joseph decided to go to Masada, Herod dismissed all of his retainers with the exception of some eight hundred soldiers, friends, and family, a smaller number that would have a better chance to hold the mountain fortress against attack (see Josephus *Antiquities* 14:355-364). Furthermore, there were not enough provisions stored at Masada to provide for nine thousand people. From Masada, Herod journeyed to Petra, the Nabataean capital, to seek assistance:

> As for Herod, the great miseries he was in did not discourage him, but made him sharp in discovering surprising undertakings; for he went to Malchus, king of Arabia (of the Nabataeans at Petra), whom he had formerly been very kind to, in order to receive (help). . . . But there came messengers from Malchus to meet him, by whom he desired to be gone, for the Parthians had laid a charge upon him, not to entertain Herod. (*Antiquities* 14:370-372)

After the Nabataeans refused to assist Herod, he fled to Rome via Egypt. In Rome, Herod was well received by Mark Anthony and Octavian. He was promised Roman financial and military assistance to defeat the Parthians and to gain control of Palestine. He remained in Rome for about one week, then he returned to Palestine to free his family and to defeat Antigonus and the Parthians. After a three-year war, Herod finally defeated the Parthians, took control of the Land, and had Antigonus assassinated. In 40 BCE he had been confirmed by the Roman Senate as king of Judea, a king in name only with no country to rule. In 37 BCE he took control of the Land and became king in reality.

5. *The Treasury at Petra. Petra, the Nabataen capital city, is located in southern Jordan. Herod sought assistance from the Nabataeans before he fled to Rome.*

Herod's reign can be divided into three very distinct periods. From 37 to 25 BCE he concentrated on domestic affairs and consolidating his power. The country had been in chaos for decades. The people needed peace and stability. During this phase of Herod's reign he executed his political enemies, created jobs for many people living in urban areas, and focused on internal and imperial politics. In 32 BCE war erupted between Octavian and Mark Anthony. Through shrewd political maneuvering, Herod managed to make each combatant feel as if he supported him against the other. As a result, when Octavian defeated Mark Anthony, Herod was rewarded for his loyalty by being given greater authority and more territory.

The second phase of the reign of Herod is a time of relative peace and prosperity (25–13 BCE). During the latter part of the first phase of Herod's reign, he initiated a massive and ambitious building program. The implementation of his building program reached its zenith here in the second phase. Many people were employed in this building program. Furthermore, Herod received vast revenues from the fertile farming lands of the Jordan Valley, the Coastal Plain, and Shephelah; from his port city in Caesarea; and from trade caravans passing through Palestine along the Via

Maris. People were working and earning money and there was, generally speaking, contentment in the Land. During this second phase, Herod's palaces in Jerusalem and Jericho were built, and the Herodion and most of the work on the Temple were complete.

The final phase of Herod's reign (13 BCE until his death in 4 BCE) was characterized by domestic decline and discontent among the people. Herod's building program became more costly just at a time when his finances began to dry up. A disastrous famine hurt his agricultural productivity. More and more commerce was done by maritime transport, diminishing the importance of the Via Maris. To finance his building program, Herod increased the taxation on the people, many of whom were unemployed. When he could not raise adequate funding, he resorted to enforced labor to complete his projects. Furthermore, as Herod aged questions about succession arose. His various wives plotted behind his back to try to secure power for their own sons. Some of them plotted against Herod himself and, upon being discovered, were executed for their subversion. He ordered his favorite wife, Mariamne, and his son Antipater executed just five days before his own death (see Josephus *Antiquities* 15:202ff.; *Wars* 1:664ff.).

Herod died in 4 BCE at his winter palace in Jericho (Tulul Abu el-Alaiq) and was taken to the Herodion for his burial. Josephus reports the following of Herod's death and burial:

> After this, the distemper seized upon his whole body, and greatly disordered all its parts with various symptoms; for there was a gentle fever upon him, and an intolerable itching over all the surface of his body, and continual pains in his colon, and dropsical tumors about his feet and an inflammation of the abdomen, and a putrefaction of his privy member, that produced worms. Besides which he had a difficulty of breathing upon him, and could not breathe but when he sat upright, and had a convulsion of all his members. . . . Yet did he struggle with his numerous disorders, and still had a desire to live, and hoped for recovery, and considered several methods of cure. . . . So Herod, having survived the slaughter of his son five days, died, having reigned thirty-four years, since he had caused Antigonus to be slain, and obtained his kingdom; but thirty-seven years since he had been made king by the Romans. . . .

After this they betook themselves to prepare for the king's funeral; and Archelaus omitted nothing of magnificence therein, but brought out all the royal ornaments to augment the pomp of the deceased. There was a bier all of gold, embroidered with precious stones, and a purple bed of various texture, with the dead body on it, covered with purple; and a diadem was put upon his head, and a crown of gold above it, and a scepter in his right hand . . . and the body was carried two hundred furlongs to Herodium, where he had given order to be buried. (*Wars* 1:656-673)

6. *The Herodion Fortress. According to Josephus, this is the burial place of Herod the Great.*

Following the death of Herod, the kingdom was divided among three of his surviving sons. Archelaus was given Judea, where he ruled from 4 BCE to 6 CE. He proved to be too ruthless and inept for the task and was replaced by a series of Roman prefects, or procurators, who ruled Judea for Rome. Herod Antipas was given the territories of Galilee and Perea. He ruled there from 4 BCE to 39 CE. Herod Antipas is the Herod who ordered the execution of John the Baptist and before whom Jesus stood trial (according to Luke). Finally, Herod Philip ruled in Gaulanitis, Batanaea, and Trachonitis from 4 BCE to 34 CE.

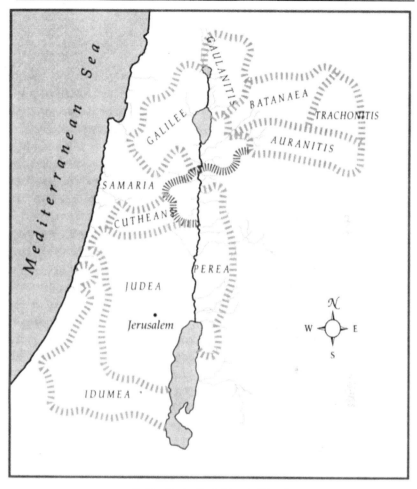

7. *Territories Ruled by the Herods*

Nazareth: The Name

The name *Nazareth* is probably taken from the Hebrew word *netzer*, which means "a shoot," and is taken from a passage found in Isaiah 11:1-2:

> A shoot shall come out from the stump of Jesse,
> and a branch shall grow out of his roots.
> The spirit of the LORD shall rest on him,
>   the spirit of wisdom and understanding,

the spirit of counsel and might,
the spirit of knowledge and the fear of the LORD.

The English letter z may be used to transcribe two different Hebrew characters. One of these Hebrew letters is known as the *zyne* and is pronounced as "z." The second letter is named *tzade* and is pronounced with a "tz" sound. During the excavations of Caesarea Maritima in 1962, under the direction of Michael Avi-Yonah, excavators discovered a Hebrew inscription on a marble fragment dating to the third century CE confirming the spelling of the name Nazareth with the Hebrew letter *tzade*, making the correct pronunciation of the village at this time "Natzareth." It is believed that the village was so named (Natzareth) because the residents considered themselves the *netzer* ("shoot") from the clan of David, from whom the Messiah would come.

We know from the writings of Epiphanius, Eusebius, Jerome, and others that the Jewish followers of Jesus were known as the Nazarene sect up until the fourth century CE.[12] Furthermore, in Acts 24:5 we find Paul being referred to as a "ringleader of the sect of the Nazarenes." Even the Talmud refers to Jesus and his followers as being the "despised shoot."[13] Our question is this: Is it possible that a Natzarene sect predated the birth of Jesus, one that thought of itself as being the vehicle through which God would establish the messianic age? The answer to this question is, perhaps, found in the Dead Sea Scrolls (1QH vi.15; vii.8, 10). Here we discover that the founder of the Essene sect thought of the movement as being the *netzer* sown by God.

Perhaps the clan of David had a similar self-understanding. It is quite likely that the residents of Nazareth were Hasidim, similar theologically to the Essenes. They were isolationists much like the modern Hasidim, marrying within the clan/sect, interacting with the outside world only when absolutely necessary. So we may conclude that the village of Nazareth was populated by an inward-focused, isolationist people who thought that the Messiah would come from within their clan. They, like the Essenes, thought that they were the sole possessors of the truth of God's law and will and that all other groups were heretical. Furthermore, we know that only two groups of people usually kept detailed genealogies: priestly families and the descendants of the house of David. (The Gospels of Matthew and Luke preserve Jesus' genealogy.)

Eusebius preserves a portion of a lost book entitled the *Epistle of Aristides,* written by a second-century follower named Africanus, which refers to the Nazarenes of this period. "A few . . . having it in their power in some other way, by means of copies, to have private records of their own, gloried in the idea of preserving the memory of their noble extraction. Of these were the above mentioned persons, called *desposyni,*[14] on account of their affinity to the family of our Savior. These coming from Nazara, and Cochaba, villages of Judea, to the other parts of the world, explained the aforesaid genealogy from the book of daily records, as faithfully as possible."[15] The Natzorean clan (or sect), as we see from Eusebius, kept a record of their genealogy, perhaps because they did expect the Messiah would come from their group. It is also possible that the people of Cochaba[16] were also members of the clan or sect of Natzoreans who were looking for the Messiah from within their own family.

Nazareth: The Village

8. The Village of Nazareth Overlooking the Jezreel Valley

The archaeological record indicates that Nazareth was a very small village during the first century. Its population was approximately 150 persons. Nazareth was located in the hills of Lower Galilee and was not a stop on any major trade route, although it was near the Via Maris.[17] The evidence also reveals that Nazareth had been occupied in the Bronze and Iron Ages, but that it was abandoned near the time of the Assyrian conquest of the Northern Kingdom (722/721 BCE) or perhaps slightly earlier at the time of the invasion of Tiglath-Pileser III in roughly 733 BCE. The Assyrians conquered most of the major cities, towns, and villages of the Northern Kingdom. Nazareth, however, was abandoned. There is no evidence of any destruction at this time. In other words, Nazareth was so small and insignificant that the Assyrians did not even bother to occupy it. The evidence further indicates that there was a habitation gap from the time of the Assyrian Conquest until the village was resettled during the Hasmonean Period.

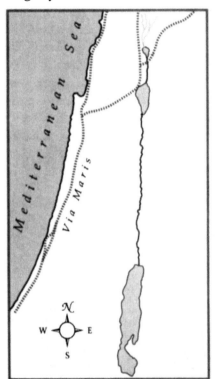

About those who settled in the village that would be named Nazareth, Bargil Pixner writes:

9. *The Via Maris, one of the most important trade routes in this part of the world.*

One can quite justly assume that Nazara-Nazareth (Little-Netzer) acquired its name from a Davidic clan, that presumably came from Babylon around the year 100 BCE. Many examples can be found of tribal or clan names being used to refer to places, e.g., Dan of the tribe Dan; Shomron (Samaria) from the clan of Shomer; Jebus (Jerusalem) from the Jebusites; Manda, north of Nazareth, in all probability from the clan of the Mandaeans.

What the original name of this location of the tribe of Zebulon may have been, is unknown to us. . . .

The findings of excavations in Nazareth allow conjectures that Nazareth was uninhabited during the Persian and early hellenistic times (8th-2nd centuries B.C.). The lack of any Assyrian, Persian, and early Hellenistic ceramic points to a long settlement gap. This absence was confirmed to the author by B. Baagatti, the excavator of Nazareth, shortly before his death in the autumn of 1990. One can surmise that this gap filled when a group of the Davidic Natzorean clan settled in the deserted village as immigrants from the Babylonian exile. Seeing that the Davidic family of Nazareth, as portrayed by the Evangelists, did not consist of the holy family but also other clan relatives (syngenies Mk. 6:4), one may well take it for granted that most of the inhabitants of Nazareth belonged to the same extended family, that is to say, to the clan of the Nazarene.[18]

Represented here were various trades, but the primary industry of the village would have been agriculture.[19] Among the other vocations one would expect to find in a small rural village

10. *Terrace Agriculture in the Kidron Valley. In biblical times, most farming was done on terraces such as these.*

would be the rabbi, tanners, shepherds, basket makers, and, of course, carpenters.[20] Furthermore, sons usually followed their fathers' occupations. This would have been true of Jesus as well. In smaller villages most of the goods used by the inhabitants would have been produced locally. Clothing was generally produced in the home for the individual family members. Each family probably had a small plot of land, usually on a terraced hillside, where they grew fruits and vegetables.[21] Because the people were very poor, usually meat would be available only on special occasions (such as a wedding). The typical daily diet would consist of bread, fruit, carob, and water.[22]

Since Nazareth was a very small village that was not located on a major trade route and was populated by an ultraconservative Hasidic sect, one can better understand Nathanael's response to Philip's announcement of the arrival of the Messiah: "Can anything good come out of Nazareth?" (John 1:46)—that backward, holier-than-thou village in the middle of the countryside!

CHAPTER TWO

PRELUDE TO MINISTRY

Childbirth

Having children has always been encouraged in Judaism; in fact, it is considered a blessing for the father and mother to have children. Rabbinic literature is clear on this matter: "No man may abstain from keeping the law 'Be fruitful and multiply' [Gen. 1:28]."[1] Even some Essenes were allowed to marry for the purpose of procreation. David Flusser, Emeritus Professor of Early Judaism and Christian Origins at the Hebrew University of Jerusalem and a prominent biblical scholar in the Land, informs us that some of these Essenes, however, were not allowed to marry until the woman had first conceived during the betrothal period:

> Josephus stresses that they did not marry, but examination of the skeletons found in the excavations have revealed, without doubt, that there were women there [at Qumran]. The Roman author Pliny also says that they did not have wives, but Josephus, who knew that some of them did, speaks of those who were married [*Wars* 2:161]. That is to say, there were those who decided that, in order for the human race not to disappear from the world, it was worthwhile to marry. I assume that fairly many did have wives, but here we should note an important phenomenon: the Essenes who did marry accepted marriage to one woman only, that is monogamy. In fact, at that time most Jews were monogamous. It is not known, for example, that any of the Sages had more than one wife, although they were permitted to do so. In contrast, for the Essenes, this was a law. They maintained that as entry into the Ark was two by two, and as Adam and Eve became one flesh

from two, it meant that the reproductive unit was monogamy. But since those who married did so only in order to "be fruitful and multiply," there was an engagement period, and only when the woman became pregnant did they marry.[2]

This practice was not exclusive to the Essenes. The Mishnah informs us that sexual activity among engaged or betrothed persons could also be found in Judea. "If in Judea a man ate in the house of his father-in-law and had no witnesses he may not lodge a virginity suit against her, since he had (already) remained alone with her" (Mishnah Ketuboth 1:5).[3] Furthermore, "Three months (of her widowhood) must pass by before the wife of the deceased brother may perform halitzah or contract levirate marriage. So, too, other widows may not (again) be betrothed or married before three months have passed, whether they are virgins or not virgins, whether they are divorced or widows, whether they were married or (only) betrothed. R. Judah says: They that had been married may forthwith be betrothed, and they that had been (only) betrothed may forthwith be married, excepting betrothed women in Judea, since (there) the bridegroom is less shamefast before her" (*Mishnah Yebamoth* 4:10).[4]

With the possibility that Joseph and Mary were from Hasidic families, similar theologically to the Essenes, and since they were more than likely Judeans, one cannot help wondering how this information might affect our understanding of the virgin birth theology of most Christian traditions. However, as Hendrikus Boers suggests, the birth narratives about Jesus are not really about the virgin birth:

> The function of all these stories is to tell who Jesus was. Divine generation stories say that he was born, not of a human father, but of God, and the infancy narratives make the reader aware that he was not an ordinary child. All of these are legends, but legends can be a powerful means of expressing the significance of a person. One can be almost certain that none of the events narrated in these stories actually happened, and yet they are the means by which New Testament Christians educated those to whom these traditions were handed down about who Jesus actually was. If we do not seek historical facts about the life of Jesus

in these stories, we will recognize in them important sources for understanding how Jesus was perceived in the communities in which they were developed and handed down.[5]

This point must not be minimized. For many people today who have a significant theological investment in the virgin birth stories, we must understand that this entire theory was a non-issue in Christianity's formative beginnings.

There were high infant and maternal mortality rates in the first century. Because delivery was sometimes difficult, midwives assisted with childbirth. The Mishnah informs us that midwives were very active and were even allowed to travel beyond the prescribed limits on the Sabbath to assist in the delivery of newborns. "They may deliver a woman on the Sabbath and summon a midwife for her from anywhere, and they may profane the Sabbath for the mother's sake and tie to the navel-string" (*Mishnah Shabbath* 18:3).[6] Also, "There was a large courtyard in Jerusalem called Beth Yaazek, where all witnesses assembled, and there the Court examined them. And they prepared large meals for them so that they might make it their habit to come. Before time, they might not stir thence the whole day; but Rabban Gamaliel the Elder ordained that they might walk within two thousand cubits in any direction. And not these, only but a midwife that comes to help a delivery . . . they, too, are deemed to be people of the city and may move within two thousand cubits in any direction" (*Mishnah Rosh Ha-Shanah*).[7] Possibly Mary would have had the assistance of a midwife during the birth of Jesus. Perhaps Mary gave birth alone. We cannot know one way or the other. However, the practice was so common and necessary that it could not have been unknown to Mary and Joseph or their families.

After the birth of a child, requirements of the law and cultural traditions needed to be fulfilled.[8] Safrai observes: "One final detail of childbirth may be mentioned: the afterbirth was not discarded, but buried, the belief being that this would help to warm the newborn baby. 'On a sabbath, the rich preserve the afterbirth in oil, and the poor in straw, but on week-days all bury the afterbirth in the ground, in order to give the earth a pledge.' Infants were swaddled and left in their cradles during the day. One passage in the Babylonian Talmud indicates that in southern Judaea it was customary to plant a cedar tree at the birth of a son and an acacia tree for a daughter; when the children were eventually married branches from these trees were used in constructing the wedding canopy."[9] Safrai goes on to report: "A clear and detailed tradition of the Temple period informs us that women did not usually go to Jerusalem following the birth of each of their children, but would rather go after a few births, bringing all the sacrifices together. The Mishnah reports that at one time the price of doves was so high Rabban Simeon ben Gamaliel ruled that a woman could fulfill with a single sacrifice her obligations for five births or miscarriages, whereupon the price of doves immediately dropped."[10]

According to Jewish Law (Leviticus 12:3), all males were to be circumcised on the eighth day of life. Thus Luke 2:21 reports that Jesus was circumcised and named on the eighth day of his life. The Talmud tells us that this was a day of great celebration that was attended by many members of the baby's family.[11] Although not mentioned in the Gospel account(s), Joseph's family from Bethlehem and Mary's family, perhaps from Jerusalem, certainly may have attended in large numbers, especially considering that this was the couple's first child. In twentieth-century Judaism, it is still the case that the circumcision of a son is a festive occasion attended by many persons, both family and friends.[12]

The Birth Narratives

Various traditions attempt to give us some insight into the announcement of Jesus' birth, Joseph and Mary's life just prior to the birth, and the family's move from Judea to Nazareth. We will briefly examine some of these traditions in the hope that this background will shed some light on later developments in Jesus' theological growth.

The author of the Gospel of Luke locates the homes of Mary and Joseph in Nazareth at the time of the announcement of Jesus' birth. We are told that Joseph's family is from Bethlehem (see Luke 2:1-4). Mary and Joseph have become engaged, and it is during this engagement period that the announcement of Mary's pregnancy is made in Nazareth.[13] How did Joseph come to be in Nazareth, and how did he meet Mary? How did he come to be engaged to Mary?

11. *Orthodox Church of Annunciation or Mary's Well. One of the traditional sites of the annunciation of Jesus' birth to Mary is "Mary's Well," found inside a Greek Orthodox Church in Nazareth.*

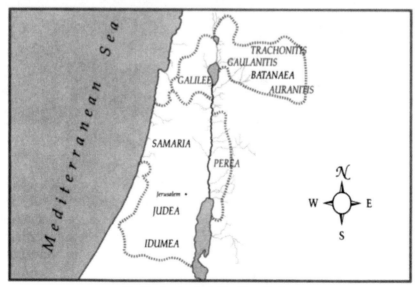

12. *Territories Ruled by Herod's Sons*

In 4 BCE, Herod the Great died in Jericho in Judea and was buried in an unmarked grave in or near the Herodion Fortress near Bethlehem. After his death three of his sons were appointed to rule in his place. Herod Antipas ruled in Galilee and in Perea, a region found on the eastern bank of the Jordan River in what is now modern Jordan.

After his appointment, Antipas chose Zippori,[14] a small city located approximately three miles (approx. five km) north of Nazareth, for his capital city, and a massive building campaign was undertaken to turn the town into a major center of government, commerce, finance, and culture in the Galilee. In order to accomplish this major expansion, construction workers would have been drawn to Sepphoris to find work. An early church tradition suggests that Joseph was one of these persons, but that he chose not to live in a booming metropolis. Instead, he resided in a small village much like his own village of Bethlehem. This nearby village was Nazareth.

13. Zippori. Perhaps the "city that is set on a hill" (Matt. 5:14) and the possible place where Josephus and Jesus worked as stone masons. This was also the seat of Herod Antipas's government in Galilee.

Another tradition of the early church suggests that Mary grew up in Zippori and that her grandparents' homes were also located in Zippori. This tradition is preserved by the Sisters of Anna, an Italian order that owns and operates a small orphanage near the ruins of Zippori. On the grounds can be found the ruins of a Crusader church that preserves a Byzantine mosaic with an Aramaic inscription, which the sisters claim comes from a Byzantine church built on the site of Mary's Zippori home. According to this tradition, Mary's father died about the time the town began to expand. Mary's mother, Anna, moved away from the town and settled in Nazareth because it was a quieter place to raise her young daughter.

14. Latin Church of the Annunciation at Nazareth

15. A Cave House in Nazareth. Houses in first-century Nazareth were hewn out of the soft limestone and resembled caves. This is the kind of house in which Jesus would have lived.

This tradition thus suggests that both Mary and Joseph settled in Nazareth about the same time and that shortly after their
arrival they met and became engaged. Luke picks up the story
from this point and leads us from Nazareth to the birth of Jesus
in Bethlehem. The critical point in this tradition is that the
Gospel has Mary and Joseph begin in Nazareth.

16. *St. Joseph's Church. This church was built over the traditional location of the*
house of Joseph.

The Gospel of Matthew offers a different account. Here the
author suggests that the family begin in Bethlehem, travel to
Egypt, and finally go on to Nazareth:

When Herod died, an angel of the Lord suddenly appeared in a
dream to Joseph in Egypt and said, "Get up, take the child and
his mother, and go to the land of Israel, for those who were seeking the child's life are dead." Then Joseph got up, took the child
and his mother, and went to the land of Israel. But when he
heard that Archelaus was ruling over Judea in place of his father
Herod, he was afraid to go there. And after being warned in a
dream, he went away to the district of Galilee. There he made his
home in a town called Nazareth, so that what had been spoken
through the prophets might be fulfilled, "He will be called a
Nazorean." (Matt. 2:19-23)

46

This passage suggests that Joseph did not relocate his family to Nazareth until after the birth of Jesus.

Yet another church tradition locates the home of Mary and her family in Jerusalem. Today, located just inside the Lion Gate (or St. Stephen's Gate) in the Old City, is found the Church of St.

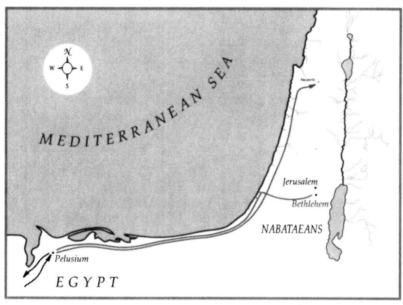

17. *Route of Mary and Joseph's Flight to Egypt and Return to Nazareth*

18. *St. Anne's Church in Jerusalem. This church was built over one of the traditional locations of Mary's childhood home, inside the Lion Gate in the Old City of Jerusalem.*

Anne, a Crusader church built over the traditional site of Mary's childhood home. This tradition corresponds to one found in the *Protevangelium Jacobi*,[15] which suggests that Mary's family lived in the Jerusalem area where her father regularly made offerings in the Temple and where Mary served as a Temple attendant until she met and was later betrothed to Joseph. Since the family did not move to Nazareth until after the death of Herod the Great (see Matthew 2:22-23), the angel's announcement of the birth must have taken place here rather than in Nazareth, or so this tradition argues.

This tradition is supported by the social custom of the day. Usually when a man married he would bring his new wife to live in the house of his father. One of the responsibilities or duties of the father was to provide a place for his sons' families.[16] The newlyweds would be provided a sleeping chamber in the house belonging to the patriarch of the extended family. If we assume that Joseph was not aged, as the *Protevangelium Jacobi* suggests, we must conclude that he would have followed this custom and brought his wife to their new home in his father's house. Perhaps, then, Jesus was born in the stable located in a cave beneath the family's house. This would afford more privacy for Mary and prevent accidental physical contact with the ritual uncleanness of childbirth. If Joseph and Mary followed the custom of the day, then Jesus must have been born in the house of his grandparents in Bethlehem.

If one had to choose which of these two stories is what really occurred, assuming that one is more correct than the other, the Matthew tradition best corresponds to the customs and culture of the day. Joseph probably did settle in Nazareth because of its proximity to Zippori and because it was a small, conservative, religiously fundamentalist village similar to his home village of Bethlehem.

Jesus' Childhood and Adolescence

For our understanding of the culture of the day, it is vital that we also understand how people lived during the first century CE. Realizing that Jesus and his family were also products of their time and environment, it would be helpful to have some sense of how the people lived and earned a living in various parts of the country, which varied depending on where one lived. The people in small villages were involved in small business or the types of commerce that would support the economy of the village. In larger cities, one would expect to find an intricate commercial complex that supported not only local business but also wider national and international trade.

Furthermore, the two dominant examples of commercial endeavor were localized also, depending on where one lived. For example, land better suited to agriculture was found in the western part of the country and near adequate water sources—thus from the Mediterranean Sea to the Central Highlands, the region in the north around the Sea of Galilee, and in the Jordan Valley. Grazing lands for sheep was found in the more arid areas of the country east of the Central Highlands and in Judea and southward.

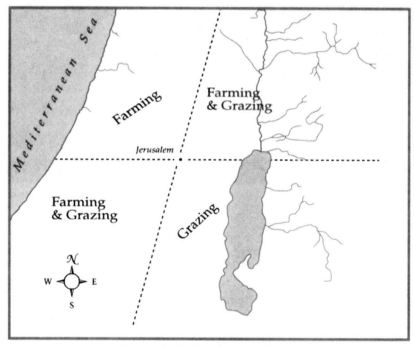

19. *Agricultural and Grazing Areas*

It is also critical for us to understand the types of houses in which people lived. This is particularly true when considering how Joseph, Mary, and Jesus lived, whether in Bethlehem or in Nazareth. The archaeological record has shown that housing styles varied from region to region. In Bethlehem the houses were usually built multistoried and over caves, which served as stables for the livestock, usually sheep; shepherds comprised the major segment of the population. Jesus' birth in a stable is not so surprising when we realize that a stable would have been a quiet, dry, and comfortable place for Mary and Joseph, away from the many people who lived in the multifamily complex above.

20. *A Cave in Bethlehem. In Bethlehem, caves like this one were used as stables for animals. Houses were built on top of such caves.*

The archaeological record in Nazareth indicates that people lived in homes hewn out of the soft limestone bedrock common to the area. In short, people lived underground. Some of the dwellings that have been excavated underneath the Church of the Annunciation have been houses with several rooms, some of which may have been inhabited by extended family members. Some were used as stables for livestock. In the back rooms have been found "kitchens," rooms with ovens in them. The family members would have slept in the room nearest to the entrance to the house.[17]

In Capernaum, Chorazim, and Bethsaida, most of the populace—except for the very wealthy—lived in houses known today as insulae. The insula was a large communal living arrangement with sleeping chambers for individual families. In most cases, extended families would occupy one insula, but this was not always the case. For example, the home in which Jesus lived in Capernaum belonged to Peter's mother-in-law; probably other disciples lived there as well.

Typically an insula included a large, open, common courtyard, where the people would gather for a visit, to eat their meals, and so forth. Adjacent to the inner wall of the courtyard was a bench where people might sit. Above the bench might be a thatched eave that would provide shade for people sitting in the courtyard. The sleeping chambers that surrounded these courtyards were too small for gatherings; their sole function was for sleeping during the winter months. In the summer, or hotter months, families slept on the roof. The usual dimensions

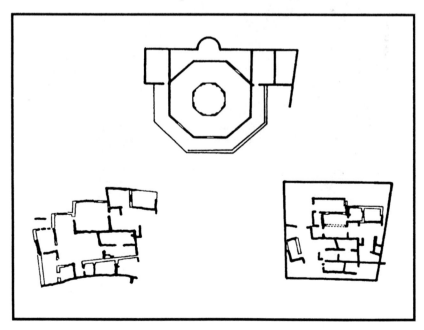

21. Drawing of an Insula

of the sleeping chambers were approximately two by three and one-half meters. Inside there would be little furniture, perhaps only a small table. People would sleep on straw mats spread on the floor, which was constructed of basalt stones. Some of these sleeping rooms had small windows to allow light into the room. During the winter months, parents would sleep with their small children, with the parents on opposite ends and the children in the middle. They would snuggle together during the cold nights and warm themselves on one another's body heat. The mother might sleep nearest to the door leading out to the oven, because she would rise early to prepare bread for the day. Few of these families had much personal property; they had few possessions to keep in these rooms. Usually the poorest people owned little more than the clothes they wore.[18]

22. *Ruins of an Insula in Chorazim*

What was Jesus' childhood like? He would have been reared just as any Jewish boy from a small, conservative village. As a young boy he would have learned Torah and the oral tradition from his local synagogue, the center of village life.

There were many laws (both oral and in the Torah) that governed the rearing of children and the behavior of children. Thus parents began early to train their children in the religious law that would govern their lives. Some of these laws were quite strict. For example, in the Torah we find:

If a man has two wives, one of them loved and the other disliked, and if both the loved and the disliked have borne him sons, the firstborn being the son of the one who is disliked, then on the day when he wills his possessions to his sons, he is not permitted to treat the son of the loved as the firstborn in preference to the son of the disliked, who is the firstborn. He must acknowledge as firstborn the son of the one who is disliked, giving him a double portion of all that he has; since he is the first issue of his virility, the right of the firstborn is his.

If someone has a stubborn and rebellious son who will not obey his father and mother, who does not heed them when they discipline him, then his father and his mother shall take hold of him and bring him out to the elders of his town at the gate of that place. They shall say to the elders of his town, "This son of ours is stubborn and rebellious. He will not obey us. He is a glutton and a drunkard." Then all the men of the town shall stone him to death. So you shall purge the evil from your midst; and all Israel will hear, and be afraid. (Deut. 21:15-21)

The responsibility for education in the home fell to both parents and also to grandparents who lived nearby. The Talmud points out how grandfathers assisted in teaching the children Torah. Both male and female children participated in the religious rituals of the home and in some of the rituals of the synagogue. At what age did they begin? Safrai writes:

Religion and society made no sharp distinction between childhood and adolescence. The Jewish practice of celebrating the Bar Mitzva when a boy reaches the age of thirteen, marking the fact that at this age he received the obligations to observe all the commandments, originated in a later period [later than first century]. In the first century both boys and girls began to participate in social life and observe the law as soon as they were mature enough to be able to perform and understand these activities. A baraita which often appears in the sources expresses this idea as follows: "A minor who is no longer dependent on his mother is obliged by the commandment to sit in a booth (during Tabernacles); if he can wave it he is obliged to take a palm branch; if he can wrap it around himself he is obliged to wear a prayer shawl; if he can care for them, his father should buy phylacteries for him; if he can talk, his father should teach him *shema* and Torah and the sacred language; . . . if he knows how to slaughter animals, his slaughtering is kosher; if he can keep his body clean, he may eat pure foods; if he can keep his hands clean, one may eat pure food from them; if he can eat . . . a piece of meat the size of an olive, one may slaughter a paschal lamb for him."[19]

Yet, age thirteen (or puberty) is the official age when a child begins to act with some independence. The Mishnah states this clearly:

A girl eleven years old and one day—her vows must be examined; if she is twelve years old and one day her vows are valid, but they must be examined throughout the twelfth year. A boy twelve years old and one day—his vows must be examined; if he is thirteen years old and one day, his vows are valid, but he must be examined throughout his thirteenth year. When they are younger than this, even though they say, 'We know in whose name we have vowed it,' or 'in whose name we have dedicated it,' their vow is no vow and what they have dedicated is not dedicated. But when they are older than this, even though they say, 'We know not in whose name we vowed it,' or 'in whose name we dedicated it,' their vow is a valid one, and what they have dedicated is validly dedicated. (Mishnah Niddah 5:6)[20]

Jesus would have conformed to these legal restrictions both in Nazareth and in Jerusalem. He would have been trained in the Law in Nazareth, under the guidance of his father and a rabbi. His paternal grandfather more probably lived in Bethlehem (if he were still alive during Jesus' childhood) and would not have participated in his childhood training. Again, we have the tradition that Mary's family lived in Zippori (see above). If this tradition is factual, Mary's family might have participated in Jesus' early training. But this is only conjecture. More likely, Luke's reporting of Jesus' encounter with the religious elders in Jerusalem (Luke 2:41-51) occurred after Jesus had reached the age of thirteen and one day.

Jesus would have followed the tradition of the day and worked in the construction industry, as had his father before him. We may safely assume that he trained as an artisan during his childhood in Nazareth and that once he reached adolescence he, like his father, went to work in Zippori. The cosmopolitan culture of Zippori would have exposed Jesus to a broader experience than that afforded by the conservative influence of Nazareth's Judaism. There is no indication that Jesus ever visited the theater in Zippori, but certainly he knew of its existence. Perhaps adolescent curiosity would have motivated him to see a play. Could Zippori with its Greek plays be a possible source of the theatrical imagery for Jesus' teaching? For example, in the Gospel of Matthew the author uses the word *hypocrite* several times in reference to people who practice their piety in public to earn the praise of others. The Greek word for *hypocrite* is defined or understood as one who acts in a play, or "playacting." Jesus condemns playacting in the comments reported in Matthew. Thus he must have had some contact with or experience of the theater in Zippori (see Matthew 5–7; 23).

The Baptism of Jesus

Local tradition in Palestine places the baptismal site of Jesus as the Jordan River, just to the north of the Dead Sea. This tradition is based, in part, on both Matthew's account of the baptism of Jesus and, to a lesser degree, that of Luke. Matthew reports that John baptizes and preaches in the Wilderness of Judea (Matthew 3:1).[21] Jesus comes to John for baptism and meets him there in the Wilderness of Judea. Immediately following his baptism, Jesus is led out into the "wilderness" (Matthew 4:1). Luke also places Jesus in the "wilderness" for the temptation experience (Luke 4:1-2).

The Gospel of John further states that the preaching and baptismal activity of John the Baptist were not restricted to Judea alone. In John 1 we are informed that priests had been sent by "the Jews" to question John:

Now they had been sent from the Pharisees. They asked him, "What then are you baptizing if you are neither the Messiah, nor Elijah, nor the prophet?" John answered them, "I baptize with

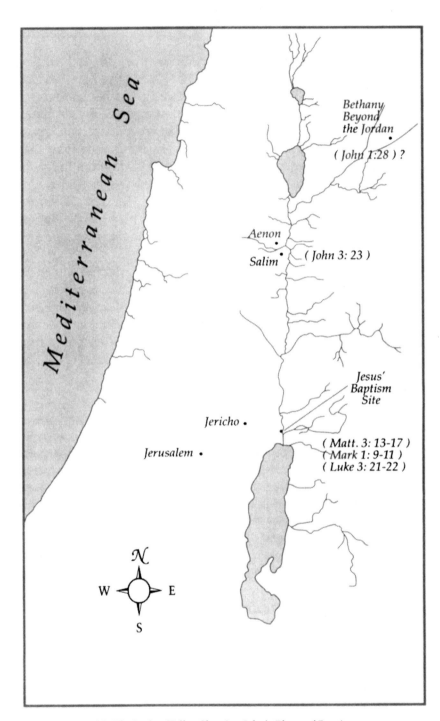

23. The Jordan Valley Showing John's Places of Baptism

water. Among you stands one whom you do not know, the one who is coming after me; I am not worthy to untie the thong of his sandal." This took place in Bethany across the Jordan where John was baptizing. (John 1:24-28)

There is considerable debate about the location of this "Bethany beyond the Jordan." Scholars in the eighteenth and nineteenth centuries thought that it might have been located on the western side of the Jordan River, in the proximity of Jericho, and that it was called Bethany beyond the Jordan to distinguish it from Bethany of Judea, found just east of Jerusalem on the Mount of Olives. However, perhaps the Greek name "Bethany" might recall or suggest the name "Batanea," the region found far to the north on the eastern side of the Jordan River in the region known as Bashan during the Old Testament period. As suggested above, this was an area settled by fundamentalists after their return from Babylon. So John the Baptist may have been preaching and baptizing in an area that espoused religious extremism. Here he would have been baptizing in the Yarmulk River or in a tributary of the Yarmulk. We also find in the Gospel of John that the Baptist was active in a place called Aenon near Salim (John 3:23). Aenon was located about eight miles (thirteen kilometers) south southeast of present-day Beth Shean. These passages all indicate that John the Baptist was active throughout the Jordan Valley preaching and baptizing in the south (Judea near Jericho), in the central part of the country (at Aenon near Salim), and in the north (at Bethany beyond the Jordan).

We know very little about the life and ministry of John. Our primary sources are the New Testament Gospels and the writings of Josephus. Josephus writes that John was respected for his piety and dedication:

Now, some of the Jews thought that the destruction of Herod's army came from God, and very justly, as a punishment of what he did against John, that was called the Baptist; for Herod slew him, who was a good man, and commanded the Jews to exercise virtue, both as to righteousness towards one another, and piety towards God and so to come to baptism; for that the washing (with water) would be acceptable to him, if they made use of it,

57

24. A Miqvah *Bath*

not in order to the putting away (or the remission) of some sins (only), but for the purification of the body; supposing still that the soul was thoroughly purified beforehand by righteousness. Now, when (many) others came in crowds about him, for they were greatly moved (or pleased) by hearing his words, Herod, who feared lest the great influence John had over the people might put it into his power and inclination to raise a rebellion (for they seemed ready to do anything he should advise), thought it best, by putting him to death, to prevent any mischief he might cause, and not bring himself into difficulties, by sparing a man who might make him repent of it when it should be too late. (*Antiquities* 18:116-118)

We have no idea why Jesus was drawn to John. Perhaps John's message drew Jesus to the Judean wilderness. Perhaps Jesus had slowly come to realize that God did not operate exclusively within one narrow-minded sect. At any rate, Jesus left Nazareth and, like many others, found his way to John. Again the Synoptic Gospels inform us that Jesus encountered John as the Baptist taught in the wilderness.

It should be noted here that John's baptism was something new and unique. Jewish people were accustomed to ritual bathing during the first century CE. This was a necessary part of daily life to restore one to a state of ritual purity from uncleanness. The bath used for these ritual immersions was known as a *miqvah*. *Miqvot* (plural) have been found in excavations throughout the Land.[22] Furthermore, John's preaching was geared to calling people to repentance in preparation for the coming kingdom of God. All hearers were given an open invitation to come for baptism. The Essenes, on the other hand, were an exclusive community. People could not join simply by a brief initiation into the sect.[23] Their invitation was conditional.

Following his baptism, Jesus went into the Wilderness of Judea for a time of self-reflection. Church tradition locates the place of testing and reflection in the area that surrounds the Wadi Qelt, located just southwest of modern Jericho. The Gospel accounts tell us that he fasted for forty days during this time of temptation and testing. A Jewish fast does not necessarily prohibit the drinking of water. Luke tells us, "And he ate nothing in those days" (Luke 4:1). None of the Gospel accounts mentions that Jesus was

25. *The Wadi Qelt. Located in the Judean Wilderness, this is the probable area where Jesus wandered in the wilderness during his time of testing.*

26. *The Jordan River*

27. *A Hill Overlooking Herod's Palace. This mountain overlooks the winter palace of Herod the Great in Jericho. Perhaps Jesus stood on a mountain like this one looking down at Herod's palace during one of the tenptations (Matt. 4:8-9).*

28. *Stones from the Wadi Qelt That Resemble Bread. These stones resemble loaves of bread, corresponding to one of the temptations of Jesus (Matt. 4:3).*

forbidden to drink. The only water source in the Wilderness of Judea approximate to the traditional site of the temptation of Jesus is a spring found at the western end of the Wadi Qelt. At Ein Qelt (*ein* means "spring"), Herod the Great had constructed an aqueduct to bring water from this spring (Ein Qelt) to his winter palace in Jericho.[24] Therefore, water flowed freely through the Wadi Qelt. The reason why this place came to be associated with the temptation of Jesus is its proximity to the southern end of the Jordan (where John baptized) and the presence of water, which Jesus could have drunk during this time of fasting, prayer, and self-reflection.

The land surrounding the Wadi Qelt is barren and intimidating. Yet, the landscape certainly suggests aspects of the temptation of Jesus. The writer of the Gospel of Matthew states, "The tempter came and said to him, 'If you are the Son of God, command these stones to become loaves of bread' " (Matt. 4:3). It is interesting that many of the stones in this area resemble loaves of fresh baked bread. We also read, "Again, the devil took him to a very high mountain and showed him all the kingdoms of the world and their splendor; and he said to him, 'All these I will give you, if you will fall down and worship me' " (Matt. 4:8-9). Perhaps Jesus was standing on a high mountain overlooking the Wadi Qelt and Tulul Abu el-Alaiq (Herodion Jericho), looking down on the palatial Herodion complex there. It is possible that Jesus was struggling with the question of what it might mean to be the Messiah. As he stood there seeing the contrast between the Wilderness of Judea and Herod's winter palace, he might have wondered if he would one day occupy such a place.

Jesus' First "Conversion" Experience and His Move to Capernaum

It was here in the wilderness that Jesus experienced his first major theological shift, or "conversion." The Greek word used in the New Testament for this experience is *metanoé* (noun: *metánoia*), which means, literally, "to turn around" or "to think differently." Jesus was reared in a very strict environment among people who thought they had been singled out as the vehicle through which God would redeem humankind. However, somewhere along the way he came to the realization that this is not how God acts—exclusively within the community of one small clan or sect. Perhaps his exposure to other peoples and philosophies in Zippori caused him to reconsider his upbringing. Perhaps it was the mysterious working of God in his life. Perhaps it was a rebellious spirit within him. Whatever the cause, Jesus certainly had a life-changing experience in the Wilderness of Judea. After this time of testing and self-reflection, he made an intentional shift from the rigid fundamentalism of his youth to a more moderate theological position. This shift is demonstrated in his move from Nazareth, the small, inwardly focused, fundamentalist village, to Capernaum (Kfar Nahum), a more moderate village closely aligned with the theology of the House of Hillel. This shift is not something that we should interpret as a minor movement on the part of Jesus. To move from Nazareth to Capernaum would be something akin to moving from a familiar setting to a place that is almost exactly opposite of all that you have ever known. It might be compared to moving from a small rural community, to an urban metropolis, where one would be exposed to things totally alien to one's upbringing and experience.

The importance of this shift or "conversion" cannot be minimized. Jesus moved theologically to the left, rejecting the strict teachings of his sect/clan to embrace a more open and inclusive expression of the Jewish faith. Certainly, Judaism has always understood itself to be the vehicle through which reconciliation would be accomplished between God and all people. Jesus rejects the strict, narrow-minded, religiously biased position of his own sect/clan in favor of the more inclusive, pluralistic position of the Pharisees of Capernaum. Even John the Baptist is too strict for Jesus as he chooses to go out on his own rather than stay with John in "Bethany beyond the Jordan" (see John 1). So here we have the first of three major shifts in the thinking of Jesus. Not only did he move away from the Hasidim, but also he embraced the more liberal of the Pharisaic schools, the House (or School) of Hillel.[25] This is suggested in the Gospel accounts of Jesus' ministry in Capernaum. The responses from the people and the religious leadership are always consistent with Hillelian thought as expressed in the Mishnah. For example, in Luke 4:31-37 we find a report about the healing of a man with an unclean spirit:

> He went down to Capernaum, a city in Galilee, and was teaching them on the sabbath. They were astonished at his teaching, because he spoke with authority. In the synagogue there was a man who had the spirit of an unclean demon, and he cried out with a loud voice, "Let us alone! What have you to do with us, Jesus of Nazareth? Have you come to destroy us? I know who you are, the Holy One of God." But Jesus rebuked him, saying, "Be silent, and come out of him!" When the demon had thrown him down before them, he came out of him without having done him any harm. They were all amazed and kept saying to one another, "What kind of utterance is this? For with authority and power he commands the unclean spirits, and out they come!" And a report about him began to reach every place in the region.

One thing we do not find in this passage is any condemnation of Jesus' healing on the sabbath. The House of Hillel placed greater emphasis on the law of loving one's neighbor than on keeping the strict laws of the sabbath. Therefore, a person had more value than laws governing one's behavior on the sabbath. To heal was a greater good than not to heal. This was a fundamental doctrine of the Hillelites and the prevailing attitude among the people of Capernaum. Jesus was not condemned for healing on the sabbath! Instead, "reports went out into every place in the surrounding region." People were positive in their reporting of this event.

So we must conclude that somewhere between his leaving Nazareth to hear John and his journey to Bethany beyond the Jordan, Jesus made the decision to effect this shift in theology. This was a major decision for Jesus. Not only was he abandoning the sect, but also he was moving away from the faith of his own family. Those who are familiar with the importance of tradition in Jewish thought will realize that this is not something that one would do casually. For Jesus, this must have been a very traumatic experience, and there would be major consequences of this action.

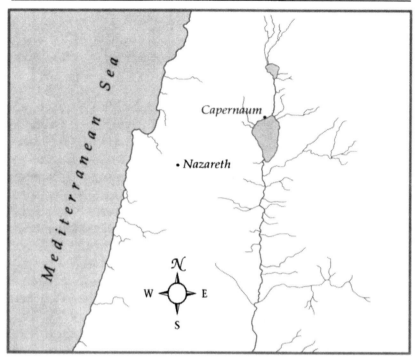

29. Capernaum and Nazareth. These two villages were not separated by a long distance but by custom, lifestyle, and religious belief and practice.

The Gospel of John does not report the baptism and temptation stories of Jesus. Instead, John takes us to Bethany beyond the Jordan, where Jesus suddenly shows up (presumably after the wilderness experience). Obviously, Jesus is seeking the Baptist and follows him from Judea in the south to Bethany in the north. John reports:

> The next day he [John] saw Jesus coming toward him and declared, "Here is the Lamb of God who takes away the sin of the world! This is he of whom I said, 'After me comes a man who ranks ahead of me because he was before me.' I myself did not know him; but I came baptizing with water for this reason, that he might be revealed to Israel." And John testified, "I saw the Spirit descending from heaven like a dove, and it remained on him. I myself did not know him, but the one who sent me to baptize with water said to me, 'He on whom you see the Spirit descend and remain is the one who baptizes with the Holy Spirit.' And I myself have seen and have testified that this is the Son of God."

> The next day John again was standing with two of his disci-
> ples, and as he watched Jesus walk by, he exclaimed, "Look, here
> is the Lamb of God!" The two disciples heard him say this, and
> they followed Jesus. (John 1:29-37)

These two disciples of John—one identified as Andrew, the
other unnamed, but perhaps the Gospel writer John himself—
come to Jesus and engage him in a conversation. (Both Andrew
and John had obviously been in the company of the Baptist and
might even have been disciples of John.) They spend the night
with Jesus in Bethany (Batanea).[26] No doubt, Jesus was still
struggling with his experience in the wilderness. He probably
had as many questions as they, and the men might have talked
late into the night. The following day, according to the Gospel
of John, Jesus and the two disciples of John travel (by land) to
Capernaum where Jesus is introduced to Simon Peter, then to
Philip and Nathanael. It was, perhaps, at this time that Jesus
took up residence in Capernaum.

Why Capernaum? Jesus probably moved here because this was
the home of his earliest followers and disciples (Andrew, Peter,
Philip, Nathanael, and the unnamed disciple, perhaps, John).
Capernaum may also have been a place where the prevailing theological attitude was more comparable to his own emerging
beliefs, understanding, and insights. Furthermore, in Capernaum
he was able to establish an association with a group of men who
were already partners in a fishing business and who probably
were living together in an insula owned by Simon's mother-in-
law (see Mark 1:29; Luke 5:10). Perhaps these men were not only
followers of Jesus but also leaders of others. We have no way of
knowing Andrew's spiritual commitment and dedication, but it
must have been considerable. It is possible that Jesus used these
first formative weeks among these men as a time for bringing
things together thelogically in his own mind.

Capernaum

Capernaum was a village (or small town) located on the
northwestern shore of the Sea of Galilee. The archaeological
record indicates that Capernaum had been occupied as early as

the Middle Bronze Period, but there is also evidence of habitation during the Late Bronze, Persian, and Hellenistic periods.[27] The town thrived until the Islamic invasion during the seventh century CE, when it was abondoned. The property then was acquired by the Franciscans in the late 1890s, and excavations began in the early 1900s.[28]

30. *Greek Orthodox Church of Upper City of Capernaum. Wealthier citizens of Capernaum would have lived near here, such as Jairus, Levi (Matthew) the tax collector, and the centurion.*

The town was separated into two sections: an upper and a lower area. The wealthy lived in the upper part of the town, now occupied by a Greek Orthodox church and monastery. Even today remains of large villas dating to the Roman Period (63 BCE–323 CE are found here. During the time of Jesus we would expect to find Jairus (the leader of the Capernaum synagogue) the Roman centurion (see Matthew 8 and Luke 7) and, perhaps, Levi the tax collector living in the upper part of the town. The lower city was inhabited by the poor, including Jesus and his disciples, who lived in the home of Simon Peter's mother-in-law. The synagogue was also located here in the lower city.

The major industry of the town was fishing. However, agriculture would have been prevalent as well. During his excava-

31. Milestones Found in the Ruins of Capernaum

tions, Corbo also found a large quantity of completed and partially completed millstones, suggesting that this was a center for the manufacture of such millstones.[29] No doubt, additional income was brought into the town as a result of its proximity to the Via Maris extension from Beth Shean to Asia, which passed just to the west of the town. Displayed today in the ruins of Capernaum is a Roman mile marker taken from the trade route near Capernaum.

Capernaum was also a frontier town, located on the border with Gaulinitis,[30] and a place for collecting various kinds of taxes imposed on the populace.[31] This would be the collection station for people crossing the border into Galilee from Gaulinitis and other countries to the north and east. Later, the manager of the local tax office would even become one of Jesus' disciples. Here Jesus would be exposed to many different people from all walks of life—people traveling with caravans on the trade route between Asia, Africa, and Europe. People also flocked to certain

32. *Roman Mile Marker. A mile marker like this one is located today in Capernaum and was found in the area near where the Via Maris passed by the Sea of Galilee.*

locations around the Sea of Galilee in search of cures for various physical ailments. The mineral baths at Hammat Tiberias and Hammat Gader were famous throughout the Roman Empire. Perhaps some of these people also came to Jesus for healing if the baths did not provide a cure.

CHAPTER THREE

THE GALILEAN MINISTRY

The Arrest of John and the Calling of the Disciples

Jesus' ministry officially began not after his birth, encounter with the elders in Jerusalem, baptism, or temptation, but after the arrest of John the Baptist. The Gospel of Mark tells us: "Now after John was arrested, Jesus came to Galilee, proclaiming the good news of God, and saying, 'The time is fulfilled, and the kingdom of God has come near; repent, and believe in the good news' " (Mark 1:14-15).

Up until this time Jesus had been preparing his disciples for their ministry together. After John was arrested, Jesus came to the Sea of Galilee and told Peter, Andrew, James, and John that it was time to get started. Again the Gospel of Mark states:

> As Jesus passed along the Sea of Galilee, he saw Simon and his brother Andrew casting a net into the sea—for they were fishermen. And Jesus said to them, "Follow me and I will make you fish for people." And immediately they left their nets and followed him. As he went a little farther, he saw James son of Zebedee and his brother John, who were in their boat mending the nets. Immediately he called them; and they left their father Zebedee in the boat with the hired men, and followed him. (Mark 1:16-20)

Some scholars have concluded, based on a limited understanding of these passages, that this is the first time that Jesus had met the disciples. However, a closer examination of the Gospels, particularly John's Gospel, makes it clear that Jesus had known the disciples earlier. Everything in the Gospel of

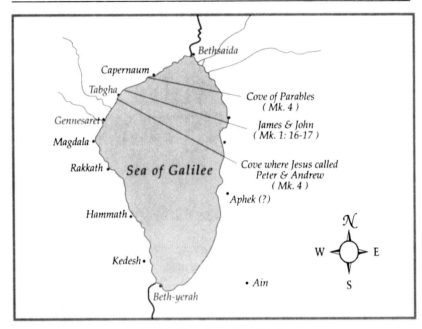

Bethsaida

Capernaum

Tabgha

Gennesaret

Magdala

Rakkath

Hammath

Kedesh

Beth-yerah

Sea of Galilee

Cove of Parables
(Mk. 4)

James & John
(Mk. 1: 16-17)

Cove where Jesus called
Peter & Andrew
(Mk. 4)

Aphek (?)

Ain

33. Fishing Coves Near Tabgha

34. Photograph of Coves. Fishing coves near Tabgha, possibly where Jesus called the disciples to follow him (Mark 1:16).

John up to 3:25 takes place before the arrest of John the Baptist.[1] This account assumes that Jesus and the disciples had already become friends, that Jesus had already moved to Capernaum, and that these men were already committed to the ministry of Jesus before Jesus called them to discipleship in Mark 1.

An early church tradition suggests that the calling of Peter, Andrew, James, and John took place in the area of Tabgha by the Sea.[2] The fishing coves of Tabgha belonged to the village of Capernaum in the first century. It is likely that those disciples who earned their living as fishermen would have used these coves. In one of these coves there is a spring that likely was the cove where James and John were cleaning and mending their nets, along with their father and coworkers, when Jesus called them to come and go with him.[3] Twentieth-century fishermen continue to use this spring, now known as Ein Nur, for these purposes.

From this time Jesus began teaching and performing miracles publicly. In the meantime, John the Baptist was imprisoned in Herod's palace at Machaerus,[4] located in modern-day Jordan near the Dead Sea. According to the Gospels of Matthew and Luke, John sent his own disciples to Jesus to ask if he was the Messiah.

> When John heard in prison what the Messiah was doing, he sent word by his disciples and said to him, "Are you the one who is to come, or are we to wait for another?" Jesus answered them, "Go and tell John what you hear and see: the blind receive their sight, the lame walk, the lepers are cleansed, the deaf hear, the dead are raised, and the poor have good news brought to them. And blessed is anyone who takes no offense at me." (Matt. 11:2-6)[5]

In short, Jesus sent a message to John that Jesus is indeed the Messiah, saying that he was doing the kinds of things that the Messiah is supposed to do.

We have demonstrated in chapter 2 that Jesus had met the disciples earlier when he was with John in Bethany beyond the Jordan (John 1:29ff.). What we see from these accounts is that there was a time of preparation between the baptism and the

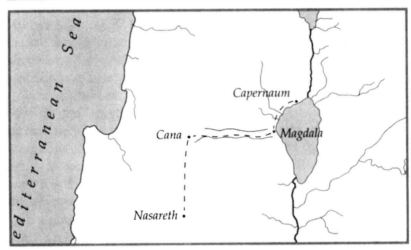

35. *Nazareth, Cana, and Capernaum. To attend the wedding in Cana, Jesus and the disciples traveled west from Capernaum, perhaps through Wadi Hamam. Mary and her family traveled north from Nazareth.*

wilderness experience of Jesus and the arrest of John the Baptist. We have no way of knowing how long this period lasted. It is possible that the preparation period lasted longer than the actual ministry of Jesus.[6] More will be said about this later. During this time of preparation, Jesus organized a small group of dedicated followers who would be actively involved in his ministry in Galilee (and beyond), moved from Nazareth to Capernaum, met and discussed theology with at least one prominent Pharisee, and prepared himself mentally and spiritually for the ministry to come. It was an important and formative part of the ministry that would have unbelievable consequences in his ministry and personal life.

We must remember that all of the events in John 1:35–3:24 (at least) happened before the ministry of Jesus began, during the preparation period.[7] Two major events in the life of Jesus took place here: (1) the wedding at Cana (2) and the encounter with the Pharisaic leader Nicodemus.

The story of the wedding in Cana is found in John 2:1-11. Cana was located north of Nazareth.[8] John's Gospel points out that not only Jesus but also his mother and brothers (and perhaps his sisters[9]) and the disciples from Capernaum were there. This could very well have been the first time that Jesus had seen his family since his baptism, temptation, "conversion," and move to Capernaum. It is further likely that this was the first time that Mary and the rest of Jesus' family met these new friends of Jesus. Therefore, there might have been some tension as they all came together in Cana. During the wedding, we are told, "when the wine gave out, the mother of Jesus said to him, 'They have no wine.' And Jesus said to her, 'Woman, what concern is that to you and to me? My hour has not yet come' " (John 2:3-4). This might have been Jesus' way to tell his mother that John the Baptist was still active and that Jesus' ministry had not yet begun. Nevertheless, Jesus performed a miracle, turning water into wine.

John's Gospel also informs us that the water Jesus used for the miracle was held in six stone jars "for the Jewish rites of purification" (v. 6). In other words, this was water for a *miqvah* bath. The *miqvah* must contain a minimum of forty *seahs* of "living water"—that is, water from a pure source not contaminated by human contact. "Anyone who came into contact with a major impurity incurred a minor impurity. All could be cleansed by a ritual bath . . . containing the forty *seahs* required for total immersion. It could hold rain-water or water drawn from a spring or stream, but not water which had been drawn or pumped. A river or the sea were of course valid. . . . The ritual bath is the main reason for the many cisterns found throughout the Land of Israel, especially near the Temple and the synagogues."[10] E. P. Sanders offers a more detailed description of the *miqvah* bath:

> The Palestinian immersion pools provide us with very interesting evidence about religious practice. . . . First of all, immersion pools are distinctive. They are neither bathtubs nor storage cisterns. . . . Immersion pools . . . were fairly large, but not large enough to store a family's water supply. Miqva'ot vary in size, but they share general characteristics: (1) They are deep, often 2 metres or 7 feet, but sometimes deeper. (2) They have a large surface area, often two metres or so in one direction, three metres or so in another (c. 7-10 ft.), though, again, many are larger. (3) Consequently they held a lot of water. A pool with a surface area of 3.6 x 2 metres and a depth of 2 metres would hold 14,400 litres of water (3,170 Imperial gallons, 3, 800 US gallons). (4) A lot of the interior space is taken up by steps, which go all the way to the bottom. (5) Frequently there is some sort of mark that divides left from right on each step; sometimes there is no mark, but there are

two sets of steps. (6) They cannot be drained: there is no plug at the bottom.[11]

The water that Jesus changed into wine had been stored for just such a *miqvah* bath. Jesus used water set aside for a ritual to produce wine for a party. This might be the Gospel writer's way of telling us that something new is happening or about to happen. Certainly this would have grabbed the attention of the first- or second-century CE Jewish reader.

After the wedding, the Gospel writer points out, Jesus returned to Capernaum with his disciples, and his mother and brothers accompanied them (John 2:12). This is a very unusual verse and one that slips by the casual reader. This is John's way of telling us that Mary and Jesus' family wanted to go to Capernaum to learn more about his new friends and their lifestyles. After all, as reported earlier, there is a great difference between life and faith in Nazareth and life and faith in Capernaum. This also demonstrates that Jesus found himself in a tension between his natural family, on the one hand, and his newly adopted "family" on the other. On several occasions his family tried to convince him to return to the faith and culture of his childhood and adolescence.[12] This conflict must have deeply saddened Jesus, and it is not resolved until just before his death, at the foot of the cross, where Jesus says to Mary, "Woman, here is your son." (John 19:26), referring to John (or the disciple whom he loved). He says to John (or the disciple whom he loved) "Here is your mother." (John 19:27). Pixner suggests that here at the cross is a reconciliation of these two diverse groups of people who loved Jesus and who were loved by him, and it is this new united family that will work together to keep the movement alive after his death and resurrection.

The second encounter found in the Gospel of John before the arrest of John the Baptist is Jesus' meeting with Nicodemus. Many pastors and theologians want to make an issue out of Nicodemus's coming to Jesus at night. However, we must not lose sight of the possibility that Nicodemus may have been too busy with his duties as a member of the Sanhedrin during the daylight hours and thus might not have had time to come earlier. In reading John's account of this meeting, we might come to the conclusion that this is a one-sided conversation, with

Jesus trying to instruct Nicodemus. However, Jesus might also have been in the position of a pupil here. He has just gone through a major shift in his own theology. He might have used this meeting with Nicodemus to further his own education and training into the theology of the Hillelians.

Following this meeting with Nicodemus, Jesus moved into the countryside of Judea and eventually returned home through Samaria. It was probably on this journey that the encounter between Jesus and the Samaritan woman, found in John 4, took place. Jesus was on his way back to Galilee (Capernaum), and he and his disciples took the shorter route to the north through Samaria. He stopped at a well near a village known as Sychar, and a woman came there to draw water at approximately noon. John reports that the disciples had gone into a nearby village to buy bread. Therefore, Jesus was alone when the woman came to draw water.

We should be aware that there are three problems with this woman. First of all, she was a Samaritan. Jews and Samaritans did not intermingle. Jewish people thought of Samaritans as being spiritual outcasts or untouchable. Second, this woman was "defiled," or was ritually unclean, because she was living in adultery. Third, cultural custom of the first century CE forbade a man to speak with a woman in public unless that woman was his wife. This custom is still practiced among the people of the Middle East, particularly among the Bedouin.[13] This helps us to better understand the disciples' reaction to seeing Jesus speak with this woman. "Then his disciples came. They were astonished that he was speaking with a woman" (John 4:27). They were as shocked to find him talking with a woman in public as with the fact that the woman was a Samaritan.

During the disciples' absence, Jesus asked this woman for a drink of water. She was shocked, of course, because she was a Samaritan and a woman. We also discover that she was an adulteress, which also disqualified her from contact with Jesus (this is why she was drawing water at noon, an uncommon hour to do so). None of this seemed to matter to Jesus, and so the woman gave him a drink. There is a brief exchange between Jesus and the woman (vv. 10-13), and then Jesus said: " 'Everyone who drinks

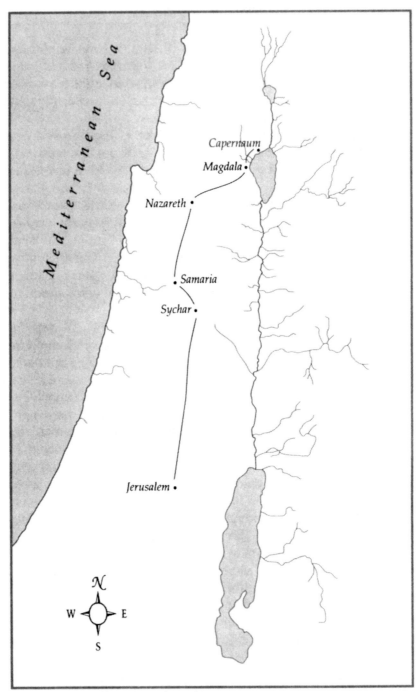

Mediterranean Sea

Capernaum •

Magdala •

Nazareth •

• Samaria

Sychar •

Jerusalem •

N
W ⊕ E
S

36. *Samaria with Sychar. In the village of Sychar, located in northern Samaria, Jesus encountered a woman at a well (John 4:5).*

of this water will be thirsty again, but those who drink of the water I will give them will never be thirsty. The water that I will give will become in them a spring of water gushing up to eternal life.' The woman said to him, 'Sir, give me this water, so that I may never be thirsty or have to keep coming here to draw water' " (John 4:13-15). This is an amazing encounter. The author of the Gospel of John assumes that we know of a social custom that anyone offering a drink of water to another person is required to be the friend of that person for one year. The offering of a drink of water and the accepting of that drink is a social contract. So when Jesus asked for a drink, even though he may really have been thirsty, he was also offering friendship to this woman who was beyond friendship. Naturally, she was shocked. "How is it that you, a Jew, ask a drink of me, a woman of Samaria?" (John 4:9). She was asking, "How is it that you, a Jew, want to be my friend, a woman of Samaria?" But Jesus took the matter a step farther by offering her friendship, not for a year, but for eternity (John 4:13-15), and the woman accepted.

In John 4:39, we read, "Many Samaritans from that city believed in him because of the woman's testimony, 'He told me everything I have ever done.' " And Jesus still wanted to be her friend, no strings attached. According to John, Jesus stayed with the Samaritans for two days and then moved on to Cana.

We have no way of knowing whether the Baptist had been arrested by the time of Jesus' meeting with the woman of Samaria. However, we must assume that either John is in prison or will be shortly by the time Jesus returns to Galilee.

Announcement in Nazareth

Following the call of the disciples, Jesus' public ministry begins with his teaching in Capernaum (Mark 1:21-22). Early in his public ministry, he decided to return to his home village of Nazareth to announce the beginning of his ministry in the local synagogue. Luke's is the only Gospel that reports this event (Luke 4:16-31). According to Luke, Jesus reads from Isaiah:

> The spirit of the Lord GOD is upon me,
> because the LORD has anointed me;

he has sent me to bring good news to the oppressed,
　　to bind up the brokenhearted,
to proclaim liberty to the captives,
　　and release to the prisoners;
to proclaim the year of the LORD's favor. (Isa. 61:1-2)

Luke reports, "And he rolled up the scroll, gave it back to the attendant, and sat down. The eyes of all in the synagogue were fixed on him. Then he began to say to them, 'Today this scripture has been fulfilled in your hearing.' All spoke well of him and were amazed at the gracious words that came from his mouth" (Luke 4:20-22). Most people often read over the words "All spoke well of him and were amazed at the gracious words that came from his mouth" (Luke 4:22*a*). Usually we tend to think that the citizens of Nazareth wanted to kill him when Jesus said, "Today this scripture has been fulfilled in your hearing" (4:21). But "all spoke well of him." This is a curious passage. Why would they speak well of him when Jesus was making a messianic statement that some might interpret as blasphemous? I believe the answer for this question is found in Isaiah 60.

We need to remember that the Natzorean sect was but one of the Hasidic sects within Judaism found in Palestine in the first century. This has been discussed in detail above. In Isaiah 60:21-22 we read:

> Your people shall all be righteous;
> 　　they shall possess the land forever.
> They are the shoot that I planted,
> 　　the work of my hands,
> 　　so that I might be glorified.
> The least of them shall become a clan,
> 　　and the smallest one a mighty nation;
> I am the LORD;
> 　　in its time I will accomplish it quickly.

"Your people shall all be righteous [Hasidim]. . . . They are the shoot [*netzer*] that I planted. . . . " Perhaps the reason why all spoke well of Jesus was because they thought he was saying to them, "Yes, I am the Messiah. Yes, you were right that the Messiah would be a shoot [a *netzer*] from our clan. And, yes, God will now establish the kingdom of God, and you will be prominent in this new order." Nazareth and the Natzorean sect were the "smallest one" that would become a mighty nation! This was God's "time" to "accomplish it quickly." Jesus quickly denounced this expectation when he said:

> "Doubtless you will quote to me this proverb, 'Doctor, cure yourself!' And you will say, 'Do here also in your hometown the things that we have heard you did at Capernaum.' " And he said, "Truly I tell you, no prophet is accepted in the prophet's hometown. But the truth is, there were many widows in Israel in the time of Elijah, when the heaven was shut up three years and six months, and there was a severe famine over all the land; yet Elijah was sent to none of them except to a widow at Zarephath in Sidon. There were also many lepers in Israel in the time of the prophet Elisha, and none of them was cleansed except Naaman the Syrian." (Luke 4:23-27)

Only when Jesus told them that outsiders would be used to initiate the kingdom of God, and not they, did they want to kill him. They had been waiting for years—and their ancestors for decades, even centuries—for God to break into history, and their entire existence was predicated on their being the clan through which God would be revealed to all of the Jewish people. Now, Jesus wipes out their hopes and desires by reporting that God would use the liberal Pharisees in Capernaum to initiate the coming kingdom and that Jesus would not allow them to use him for their own selfish purposes. In short, Jesus would not allow himself to be used by members of his clan and village for their own political and religious agenda.

Following the announcement in Nazareth, Jesus returns, with his disciples, to Capernaum, where his ministry begins vigorously and his popularity begins to grow.

Early Ministry

Mark and Luke report that at the beginning of Jesus' ministry there was a miraculous healing in the synagogue in Capernaum (see Mark 1:21-28; Luke 4:31-37). These passages report a healing in the synagogue on the sabbath. Missing from these accounts is any condemnation of Jesus for violating the sabbath. How can this be?

The answer is quite simple. The village of Capernaum was theologically accommodating to the House (or School) of Hillel, the more moderate division of the Pharisees. For the House of Hillel, the laws of loving God and loving one's neighbor took precedence over all other laws, including restrictions concerning the sabbath:

> Jesus was scrupulous in keeping the Jewish commandments. It is to be expected that the New Testament documents, written as they were in times of tension between Judaism and the Church, made a point of emphasizing that Jesus was on the side of those who abolished, partly or wholly, the commandments of the Torah. For example, in the story about the washing of hands, we have a quotation from Isaiah concerning 'teaching as doctrines the commandments of men' (Mark 7:7), where the quotation is taken from the Greek translation of Isaiah, and we can already detect a foreign influence in it. The whole passage is influenced by the doctrines of Paul, and it therefore expresses an apparent contradiction between the words of the living God as they appear in the Bible and the tradition of the Elders of the Jews (Mark 7:8).
>
> This raises the problem whether Jesus did away with the rulings of the Sages and put an emphasis only on the Written Law. This idea, which appears later in the writings of the Church Fathers, contains an absurdity-for if that had been the case Jesus would have been close to the Sadducees, and we know that he was in no way close to them. It is also clear that had Jesus lived only by the dictates of the Written Law, he would have been more stringent in certain areas (as were the Sadducees) in which we know that he was not stringent at all, and in which the Sages, too, were not stringent. When we examine Jesus' position on matters of Jewish Law, it appears that on some things he accepted the view of the more stringent authorities—the School of Shammai—and on the others, especially matters of ideology, he was closer to the School of Hillel, whose motto was 'Thou shalt love thy neighbor as thyself.'[14]

The House of Hillel was not as strict concerning sabbath laws as was the House of Shammai. Jesus was permitted to heal on the sabbath and without condemnation. In fact, he was praised for his abilities in villages where the House of Hillel was dominant. Only in villages where Shammai theology was dominant would he have been condemned for healing on the sabbath.[15]

According to Mark 1:32, the following day Jesus went out to pray in a place referred to as "a lonely place." There is a tradition in the Land that here Jesus went to the Eremos Heights, a mountain overlooking Tabgha and the Sea of Galilee, and that this became a favorite place for Jesus when he wanted to be alone.[16]

Mark reports the healing of a leper in this place of retreat.[17] An early Christian tradition locates this miracle at a site known as the "Bath of the Leper," located just north of the Primacy Church at Tabgha. Following this healing, Jesus returns to Capernaum.

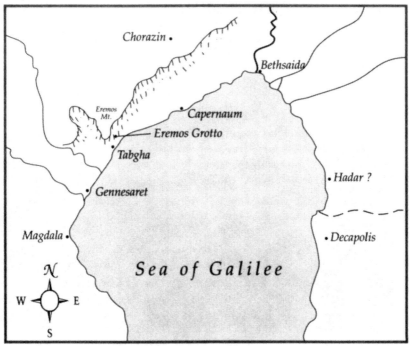

37. The Eremos Heights

In Capernaum, Jesus returns to the insula of Peter's mother-in-law. Once people realize that he is at home, they come in mass to hear his teaching and to experience his healing powers. One group comes to the house and removes a portion of the roof to lower a paralytic man to Jesus. In our culture, people may think of the removal of a roof to allow the paralyzed man access to Jesus as a major undertaking. But our understanding of how an insula functioned helps us to realize that Jesus was teaching in the courtyard, which had no roof per se.[18] Therefore, it was not such a chore to remove the thin thatched roof above the head of Jesus as he spoke with the people. This in no way diminishes what happened. It simply helps us to understand better what happened in its context.

By Mark 2, Jesus is gaining renown for his healing power and his message. Crowds gathered around him whether he was in Capernaum or by the Sea of Galilee. The more people heard the more they wanted to hear and know. This reached a climax when Jesus attempted speak to the people in Mark 4.

In Mark 4, we see that Jesus' popularity is steadily growing.

38. Eremos. A view from the Eremos Heights (a lonely or quiet place), perhaps used as a place of solitude for Jesus.

He is about to teach a group of people, but the crowd is so large he is forced to get into a boat and teach from the water. The traditional location of the place from which Jesus teaches in a boat is known colloquially in Galilee as the Cove of the Parables. This fishing cove is found about halfway between Capernaum and Tabgha. How did this cove come to be associated with Mark 4? The land here slopes gradually to the Sea of Galilee while the surrounding hillside forms a natural, horseshoe shaped theater where many people might gather. Tests conducted here have shown that the acoustics are almost perfect; someone speaking from the water's edge or from a boat near the shoreline can be heard clearly without electronic amplification for over one hundred meters. Thus this would have been a likely place for Jesus to have preached to a large crowd of people and still be in a boat in fishing waters of the village of Capernaum.[19]

39. *The Cove of the Parables. Jesus taught the parables of Mark 4 in a boat near the shore of the Sea of Galilee. This cove is a possible location due to the excellent natural acoustics found here.*

Some of the more familiar parables of Jesus are set in this location. Here, for example, he speaks of the sower who scattered seeds on various types of soil. The area here contains all of the types of soil, good and bad, mentioned by Jesus in the story. Here we find paths, rocky ground, thorns, and very good and fertile soil. The hearers would have been able to quickly relate to Jesus' message and the symbolism he suggests. Here we also find the parable of the mustard seed. Perhaps in antiquity the bush that is known colloquially today as the mustard bush was found here, but none are found here today. Most of the plants identified as such are found today in Judea in the south.

In Mark 4:35, we see that Jesus faces a dilemma. After the teaching has ended he is faced with two choices: (1) He may return to the land (the bank) where all of the people are gathered, or (2) he may travel by boat to some other destination. Mark reports that Jesus chooses the latter. Here we find a phrase that has a distinctive meaning. Jesus says to the disciples, "Let us go across to the other side" (Mark 4:35*b*). In the first century, for those who lived around the Sea of Galilee, the "other side" always referred to the Gentile side of the lake, to the Decapolis. The "other side" should be contrasted with "our side," although we never read the words *our side* in the Gospels. For people living here in the first century CE this fact was understood. Our side was the Jewish, kosher, religiously correct side. The "other side" is where we would find the pagan, idolatrous, nonkosher Gentiles with whom Jews were to have no contact. Contact with Gentiles would place one in the state of ritual impurity:

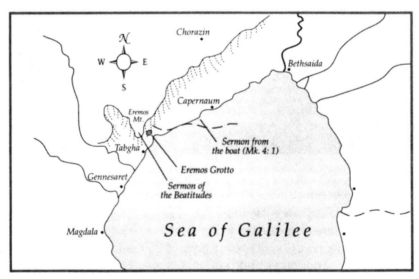

40. *Map of the Cove of the Parables*

The question of the ritual purity and impurity . . . was a major issue in the Temple era and in tannaitic times . . . we know from many regulations, especially those dealing with practical matters, and as we learn from Josephus, Philo and the New Testament, the laws of purity were widely observed. Some tried to restrict their ambit, but others to enlarge it, aiming at raising all Israel to the same level of holiness as the priests. The Sadducees maintained that purity was only for the latter, while some at least of the Pharisees held that it should be preserved by all who were willing to accept the obligation, though not necessarily incumbent on all Israel. The Essenes insisted on the full rigour of the law for all their groups, and ritual purity was one of their priorities. We list here the main grounds for ritual impurity, starting with the least serious.

1 The male sexual act. This affected both the man and the woman after intercourse. They had to take a bath and were only purified at sunset.

2 The carcass of animals, except "pure" animals killed by men and forming lawful food. This impurity also lasted till sunset.

3 A flux from a man or a woman, a woman during her period and during childbirth. The impurity lasted seven days after the disappearance of the symptoms. The purification, except in the case of the woman's period, demanded the offering of sacrifice, the minimum being two doves.

4 Contact with leprosy. This rendered a person impure for seven days, and a sacrifice had to be offered after the priest had verified the cleansing. The Torah gives details of the rite of purification, which include sprinkling with various fluids.

5 A corpse. This impurity was cleansed by the water with which the ashes of the red heifer had been mingled.

These are in the Torah. Oral law added: the non-Jew, his main residence, land outside the Land of Israel and idolatry. These were sources of impurity because of their connection with paganism though other reasons are given in later sources.[20]

With respect to the impurity of Gentiles, the Mishnah relates, "The school of Hillel say: He that separates himself from the uncircumcision is as one that separates himself from the grave" (Mishnah Pesahim 8:8).[21] Furthermore, in the book of Acts Luke writes, with respect to Peter's response to visiting the Gentile Cornelius, "You yourselves know that it is unlawful for a Jew to associate with or to visit a Gentile" (Acts 10:28).

87

So we see that Jewish interaction with Gentiles not only was discouraged, but also such contact would cause a Jewish person to become ritually defiled. Yet, Jesus says to his disciples in Mark 4:35, "Let us go across to the other side." Certainly the disciples would have heard these words with concern, doubt, or perhaps caution. They knew that it was forbidden to travel to a place where Gentiles lived and where idolatry was practiced. Perhaps they whispered among themselves that Jesus should not go there. Yet, Mark records that they nevertheless moved on to the Decapolis. The modern reader must understand that the purpose of this journey to the Decapolis was not ministry, but rather out of Jesus' desire to find a quiet place where he and his disciples could rest in peace away from the ever-growing crowds who sought to see and hear Jesus. Thus Jesus went to the other side to escape the crowds on the shore of the Sea of Galilee.

Jesus' first "conversion," his first *metanoé* experience, was from exclusive to inclusive Judaism. We must not forget that he declared himself to be the Jewish Messiah and that his ministry was confined to the Jewish people of the first century. Matthew writes, "These twelve Jesus sent out with the following instructions: 'Go nowhere among the Gentiles, and enter no town of the Samaritans, but go rather to the lost sheep of the house of Israel' " (Matt. 10:5-6). And, again, "I was sent only to the lost sheep of the house of Israel" (Matt. 15:24). Even when he was faced with the opportunity of healing a Gentile (see Luke 7) he was reluctant to do so, and the elders of the synagogue at Capernaum had to convince Jesus that this was an appropriate action on his part. Even the Roman centurion knew that Jesus did not want to have contact with Gentiles, "And Jesus went with them, but when he was not far from the house, the centurion sent friends to say to him, 'Lord, do not trouble yourself, for I am not worthy to have you come under my roof; therefore I did not presume to come to you. But only speak the word, and let my servant be healed' " (Luke 7:6-7). Jesus was obviously moved by the faith of this Gentile. He says, "I tell you, not even in Israel have I found such faith" (v. 9). Jesus had no interest in ministry among the Gentiles, not even in his home village. We must understand that this journey to the Decapolis was for rest and not for ministry.[22]

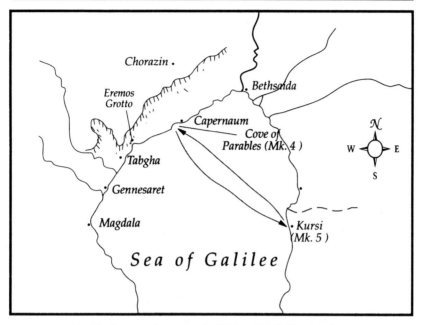

41. *The Journey Across to the "Other Side," Showing Kursi*

42. *The Kursi Ruins. This Byzantine monastery was built over the traditional site of the miracle of the swine (Mark 5:1ff.).*

89

When Jesus and the disciples landed in the Decapolis they were met by a man possessed with a demonic spirit and who was living in a cemetery.[23] Mark reports that Jesus cast the demon out of the man and into a heard of swine grazing in the general area of the cemetery. The swine ran into the Sea of Galilee, and the herdsmen ran to the nearest city (Hippos, one of the cities of the Decapolis) and reported to the owners what had happened. Mark informs us that a large contingent from the city confronted Jesus and, when they saw what had happened, asked him to leave.

Theologically two major themes are present here in this story. The first is a social gospel theme that deals with the conflict between the interests of big business and the interests of the kingdom of God. The owners of the swine herd, who have lost considerable property, asked Jesus to leave. For them, lost property was more important than the restoration of one of their own people. Second, this episode contains an evangelism theme. When the young man asked Jesus to accompany the group back to "our side," Jesus declined. Mark tells us that Jesus encouraged the man to stay in the Decapolis with the following instructions, "Go home to your friends, and tell them how much the Lord has done for you, and what mercy he has shown you" (Mark 5:19). Why did Jesus decline the offer? It is obvious that the reason why Jesus would not allow this man to join the group going to Capernaum was due to his being a Gentile. The fact that Jesus asked him to practice evangelism in the Decapolis is secondary. Jesus, in assigning the man a ministerial task in the Decapolis, demonstrates not only his compassion for the man, but also his sensitivity for the disciples and the people at home in Capernaum who would have been placed in a compromising position of accepting Jesus' new disciple from the "other side."

This is Jesus' first journey to the Decapolis and away from Capernaum after the beginning of his ministry. We must not lose sight of the fact that he did not go there for ministry but for rest away from the crowds. His understanding of his ministry, as seen in his comments regarding to the recipients of his ministry, was that he would be the Messiah for the Jewish people— and for them alone.

After Jesus arrived back in Jewish territory, he was met, per-haps, in the "Cove of the Parables," from the place where he departed to the "other side," by the leader of the synagogue of Capernaum, Jairus, and others who saw him returning. Jairus informed Jesus that his young daughter was quite ill and asked for Jesus to heal her. Jesus assented, and the crowd moved toward Capernaum, about one mile away to the north.

The Woman with the Hemorrhage

As the group walked toward Capernaum, Jesus encountered a woman who had had a "flow of blood," a hemorrhage, for twelve years. Mark reports:

> A large crowd followed him and pressed in on him. Now there was a woman who had been suffering from hemorrhages for twelve years. She had endured much under many physicians, and had spent all that she had; and she was no better, but rather grew worse. She had heard about Jesus, and came up behind him in the crowd and touched his cloak, for she said, "If I but touch his clothes, I will be made well." Immediately her hemor-rhage stopped; and she felt in her body that she was healed of her disease. Immediately aware that power had gone forth from him, Jesus turned about in the crowd and said, "Who touched my clothes?" And his disciples said to him, "You see the crowd pressing in on you; how can you say, 'Who touched me?' " He looked all around to see who had done it. But the woman, know-ing what had happened to her, came in fear and trembling, fell down before him, and told him the whole truth. He said to her, "Daughter, your faith has made you well; go in peace, and be healed of your disease." (Mark 5:24-34)

Safrai relates that in the rabbinic tradition of the Mishnah anyone with a bodily discharge was considered to be in a state of ritual impurity. Seven days without the discharge must pass before the person could even begin the rituals of purification. The Torah says:

> If a woman has a discharge of blood for many days, not at the time of her impurity, or if she has a discharge beyond the time of

her impurity, all the days of the discharge she shall continue in uncleanness; as in the days of her impurity, she shall be unclean. Every bed on which she lies during all the days of her discharge shall be treated as the bed of her impurity; and everything on which she sits shall be unclean, as in the uncleanness of her impurity. Whoever touches these things shall be unclean. . . . Thus you shall keep the people of Israel separate from their uncleanness. (Lev. 15:25-31)

Needless to say, the woman was desperate, even willing to risk violating Jewish law by touching a person while she was in a state of ritual impurity. But we must remember that Mark reported that the woman had spent all of her money and was in a worsening condition. With that information, we may better understand why she was so determined to do whatever she could to alleviate her condition.

In Matthew's version of this story, the woman with the hemorrhage touches the "fringe" of Jesus' garment (Matt. 9:18-22). Luke also uses the word *fringe* in describing the place that the woman touched (Luke 8:43-48), and Mark mentions that others want to touch the fringe of Jesus' garment (see Mark 6:56). We must ask ourselves what is going on here. Which garment worn by a Jewish man has a fringe? The answer is the *tallit*.

The *tallit*, or prayer shawl, was worn by all religious men in the first century CE. Jewish men were (and are) required to wear one to help them remember the Law: "The LORD said to Moses: Speak to the Israelites, and tell them to make fringes on the corners of their garments throughout their generations and to put a blue cord on the fringe at each corner. You have the fringe so that, when you see it, you will remember all the commandments of the LORD and do them, and not follow the lust of your own heart and your own eyes" (Num. 15:37-39).

On the corners of the *tallit* would be attached the fringes (known as *tzitzit*) required in the Torah. As mentioned, this garment was (and is) one of the most important pieces of clothing for a religious/orthodox Jewish man:

Although in ancient times four-cornered garments or robes were common, the development of clothing not having four corners would have rendered this mitzvah totally obsolete, with the full sanction of the law. To prevent the total disappearance of a mitzvah that possessed such great symbolic significance (since it serves as a reminder to observe all the commandments), the Sages encouraged the wearing of specially-made four-cornered garments so as to provide the opportunity to observe and implement the commandment.

Says Maimonides: "Although one is not obligated to buy a garment and wrap himself in it just so as to provide it with fringes, it is not proper for a devout or pious person to exempt himself from observing this precept. He should strive to wear a garment that requires fringes so as to perform this precept. And during times of prayer, one should take special care to do so." [24]

In the first century CE the *tallit* symbolized three things about the owner. First it was a symbol of the wearer's status. The Law required the tassels in the corners (the *tzitzit*) to be blue in color, so at least one blue thread must appear in the tassels in each corner. (See Mishnah *Menahoth* 4:1.) The dye used for the blue color was obtained from the fluid or blood of a small, rare snail. Because these snails were small, great quantities of them were needed in order to produce a sufficient amount of dye. This fact added to the rarity of these snails increased their value, making the production of blue dye very expensive. Since most of the people were poor they could not afford to dye all of the required tassels in the corners of the *tallit*. Thus a rabbinical interpretation of the written Law allowed poorer people to dye only a portion of their tassels blue. But the more blue that was found in one's prayer shawl, the higher status one had in the community. These blue tassels became such a symbol of status that eldest sons would inherit their father's prayer shawls and incorporate their father's blue threads into their own *tallit*.[25]

Second, the *tallit* (or *tzitzit*) also symbolized a person's authority. It was the custom for a wealthy person to wear a family signet ring. When finalizing a business transaction, the person would make an impression of this signet ring in a clay tablet. For the poor, who had no rings, the tassels of the *tallit* would serve the same purpose. When a transaction was being completed the people involved would wrap the tassels around their fingers and press them into the clay tablet, thus authorizing the transaction's completion. The Mari tablets report that when a prophet offered a prophecy and an interpretation to a king in ancient times, the prophet would be required to give to the king a piece of his tassel and a lock of his hair as a guarantee that the prophecy and interpretation were true. In 1 Samuel 18:1-4 we read: "The soul of Jonathan was bound to the soul of David, and Jonathan loved him as his own soul. Saul took [David] that day and would not let him return to his father's house. Then Jonathan made a covenant with David, because he loved him as his own soul. Jonathan stripped himself of the robe that he was wearing, and gave it to David, and his armor, and even his sword and his bow and his belt." Perhaps the writer is referring to the *tallit* when he mentions that Jonathan gave David his robe. In giving David his *tallit*, Jonathan would symbolically be giving David authority as a son of Saul in the house of the king.

Third, the *tallit* was a symbol of the covenant, of covenant election and holiness. The Torah says that the *tallit* would be worn to help the men of Israel remember the Law. The Torah also says, "Now therefore, if you obey my voice and keep my covenant, you shall be my treasured possession out of all the peoples. Indeed, the whole earth is mine, but you shall be for me a priestly kingdom and a holy nation" (Exod. 19:5-6). To demonstrate this holiness, this affirmation of being a member of the covenant people, the men of Israel would wear the prayer shawl dyed God's color, blue.

One last comment, before returning to Jesus' encounter with the woman with the hemorrhage: there was an oral tradition that prohibited a person from touching the *tallit* of someone who was not a member of one's own family. In other words, it was against the law for the woman to touch Jesus not only because she was defiled, but also because she was not of his family.

When the woman heard that Jesus was coming she decided to try just to touch the fringe of his garment; if only she could touch his holiness, authority, or status, she might be made well. This is what happened, according to the report in Mark and Matthew. Yet, after she was caught violating the Law, instead of admonishing her, Jesus called her "Daughter," thereby telling her that she was indeed in his family and invited to touch him.

94

Jesus would certainly have worn a *tallit*. In Matthew he says that he did not come to destroy the Law, and he affirms that he himself is subject to the Law. Knowing how the *tallit* was used helps us to have a clearer understanding of what happened between Jesus and this woman.

Following the encounter with the woman with the hemorrhage, Jesus went to Capernaum, where he ministered to the daughter of Jairus. When he and the disciples arrived, they were informed that the girl had died and that Jesus should not be troubled further. Jesus says, "Why do you make a commotion and weep? The child is not dead but sleeping" (Mark 5:39). Mark writes that the girl is in fact dead and that Jesus performs a miracle in bringing the girl back to life. Naturally, this was something incredible for the people of this village and this would make Jesus even more popular; greater crowds flocked to hear him teach and brought their sick for him to touch.

The First Miracle of Multiplication

In Mark 6, Jesus prepares to send his disciples out on their first missionary journey:

> He called the twelve and began to send them out two by two, and gave them authority over the unclean spirits. He ordered them to take nothing for their journey except a staff; no bread, no bag, no money in their belts; but to wear sandals and not to put on two tunics. He said to them, "Wherever you enter a house, stay there until you leave the place. If any place will not welcome you and they refuse to hear you, as you leave, shake off the dust that is on your feet as a testimony against them." So they went out and proclaimed that all should repent. (Mark 6:7-12)

In this passage, Jesus is referring to first-century hospitality customs. During this period there were five traditional acts, or gifts, of hospitality people were required to offer to a guest in their home, once that person had crossed the threshold into the house. The five acts of hospitality were (1) offering a drink of water; (2) washing the feet of the guest; (3) greeting the guest with a kiss; (4) anointing or washing the head; (5) and offering the guest something to eat.[26] Jesus knew that the disciples would be met with hospitality wherever they went. Therefore, they need not take anything with them on their journey.[27] Should they happen upon a village where they were not received appropriately, they were to leave that place.

When the disciples returned (Mark 6:30), they were anxious to tell Jesus all they had experienced. Jesus, sensing that they needed some rest and quiet time, told the disciples to go to the Eremos to rest. So they traveled from Capernaum to the Eremos by boat. However, the people discovered where Jesus and the disciples were going, so when they arrived in the coves near Tabgha, at the foot of the Eremos Heights, they found the crowds waiting for them.[28] Mark writes, "As [Jesus] went ashore, he saw a great crowd; and he had compassion for them, because they were like sheep without a shepherd" (Mark 6:34). Jesus and the disciples could simply have taken the boat to another destination. But because of Jesus' compassion and sensitivity, he went ashore to teach the people.

Following the day of teaching, as evening approached, we are told that the disciples wanted to send the people home: "When it grew late, his disciples came to him and said, 'This is a deserted place [the Eremos], and the hour is now very late; send them away so that they may go into the surrounding country and villages and buy something for themselves to eat' " (Mark 6:35-36). At this point, we have the first miracle of multiplication.[29] The Gospel of John reports the reaction of the people to this miraculous feeding: "When Jesus realized that they were about to come and take him by force to make him king, he withdrew again to the mountain by himself" (John 6:15). The Gospel of Mark adds that Jesus instructed the disciples to leave that place quickly, probably because Jesus was aware of the danger of this kind of talk. He instructed the disciples to get into their boats and go by sea to Bethsaida.

Since the beginning of Jesus' ministry, following the arrest of John the Baptist and his subsequent execution, his popularity had grown steadily. People were obviously looking for a charismatic leader, religious or civil, and John the Baptist apparently satisfied this need among the people. Jesus, too, must have inspired hope, not only through his performing miracles, but also in his teach-

43. From the Eremos Heights there is a panoramic view of the Sea of Galilee

ing. We must assume that as his popularity and fame grew, more people came to see and to hear him, why they would run around the lake to meet him (Mark 6:34), and why they would stay with him for such a long time, even past mealtime (Mark 6:35ff.). The danger with this growing popularity was that Jesus attracted increasingly larger crowds, and with these large crowds would come the possibility of political unrest. His ability to attract large crowds was John's real threat to Herod Antipas and Rome as well. After John's arrest and execution, many of his followers, no doubt, turned to Jesus. Luke hints at Herod's desire to stop Jesus before he gained the notoriety of John: "At that very hour some Pharisees came and said to [Jesus], 'Get away from here, for Herod wants to kill you' " (Luke 13:31).

Jesus' fear of this talk of revolution was well founded. Neither Herod nor Rome would tolerate either this kind of talk or large gatherings and demonstrations. Jewish historians record several incidents of revolutionary activity during the first century CE, all crushed by Rome. Luke further records examples of men who served as leaders of revolts in the first century CE in the speech of Gamaliel:

"Fellow Israelites, consider carefully what you propose to do to these men. For some time ago Theudas rose up, claiming to be somebody, and a number of men, about four hundred, joined him; but he was killed, and all who followed him were dispersed and disappeared. After him Judas the Galilean rose up at the time of the census and got people to follow him; he also perished, and all who followed him were scattered. So in the present case, I tell you, keep away from these men and let them alone." (Acts 5:35-38)

When the people decided to make Jesus king by force, his reaction was to send the disciples away, then to dismiss the people, and finally he went up on the Eremos Heights alone. Mark reports that while Jesus was there praying he saw the disciples struggling. "He saw that they were straining at the oars against an adverse wind" (Mark 6:48).[30] Mark goes on to report that Jesus, seeing his friends in distress, went out to them, walking on the water, and calmed the storm.

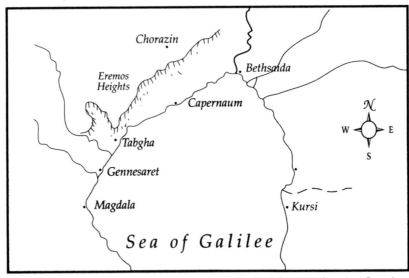

44. *The Sea of Galilee from Eremos. Jesus and the disciples were forced to flee when the people wanted to make him king by force. His disciples attempted to reach Bethsaida by boat, but landed in Gennesaret instead. Eventually, they were forced to flee to Phoenicia, to the region of Tyre and Sidon.*

The boat landed at Gennesaret. Therefore, Jesus and the disciples were still in the area where people wanted to make him king by force. Certainly Jesus wanted to get away from this area because of the danger. After a short verbal exchange with some

Pharisees, Jesus and the disciples were able to leave this area and the danger and find refuge far to the north in the region of Tyre and Sidon, in present-day Lebanon.

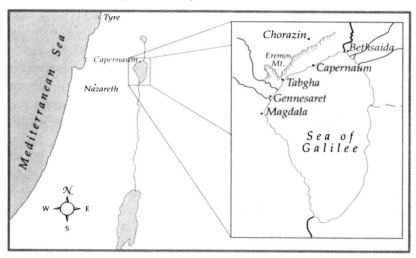

45. *Eremos, Bethsaida, Gennesaret, Tyre, and Sidon*

Jesus' Second "Conversion" Experience

Mark's account of this episode states that Jesus wanted to keep a low profile in the region of Tyre and Sidon:

> From there he set out and went away to the region of Tyre. He entered a house and did not want anyone to know he was there. Yet he could not escape notice, but a woman whose little daughter had an unclean spirit immediately heard about him, and she came and bowed down at his feet. Now the woman was a Gentile, of Syrophoenician origin. She begged him to cast the demon out of her daughter. He said to her, "Let the children be fed first, for it is not fair to take the children's food and throw it to the dogs." But she answered him, "Sir, even the dogs under the table eat the children's crumbs." (Mark 7:24-28)

Matthew's version of the story reports that Jesus also said, "I was sent only to the lost sheep of the house of Israel" (Matt. 15:24).

Jesus initially refused to help the poor woman, and he actually insulted her, calling her a dog.[31] The woman's response to Jesus' initial refusal of assistance had a major impact on Jesus' own perception of his ministry. From the beginning of the ministry and, perhaps, before, Jesus would have thought of his mission as being directed to Jewish people exclusively. His first "conversion" experience was his transformation from the narrow-mindedness of the Hasidim and the Natzorean sect to the more progressive and moderate position of the House of Hillel. In other words, this shift was from exclusive to inclusive Judaism. After the encounter with the Syrophoenician woman, we see a shift from inclusive Judaism to Jesus' expanding his mission even to the Gentiles.

In Mark 7:31ff., Jesus very intentionally returns to the Decapolis. We should remember that his first journey to the Decapolis was for rest away from the crowds (see Mark 4–5). The healing of the demoniac in the area of the ruins of Kursi was simply his response to a man in need and not a signal that the ministry would be broadened. However, he returned to the Decapolis, but this time as an extension of his own mission/ministry.

When Jesus arrived in the Decapolis he performed the miracle of healing a man who was hearing impaired. Following this (Mark 8) he taught a large crowd of people. The man from whom a demon had been exorcised in Mark 4 had been instructed by Jesus to stay in the Decapolis and to tell people what God had done for him. The throng of Gentiles who met Jesus no doubt had heard the testimony of this man, and they were anxious to see and hear him for themselves. No doubt when word of Jesus' return to the Decapolis was announced, these people gathered quickly. Mark reports that this crowd stayed with Jesus for three days without anything to eat. Finally, a second miracle of multiplication is reported on the Gentile side of the lake.

The Second Miracle of Multiplication

Consider for a moment that this second miraculous feeding, the feeding of the four thousand, is a historical event. Would any political or theological reasons influence Jesus' teaching here and the subsequent miracle? Perhaps. If we assume that Jesus first understood his mission as extending to the Jewish people alone and later changed his mind and intentionally extended the ministry to the Gentiles, then we have a basis to believe that Mark's report may be more credible than biblical criticism has supposed. Through the second "conversion" experience, Jesus realized that the Gentiles also deserved to be both recipients and partners of his mission, his ministry. Jesus had a change of mind, a change of heart. Thus his intentional journey back to the Decapolis was prompted by the new awareness of this expanding ministry.

The possibility of two miraculous feedings is also supported by looking at the types of baskets used to collect the leftovers from the meals. After the first miracle, twelve baskets of food are left over. The number of baskets are obviously related to the twelve tribes of Israel. Perhaps the symbolic message is that all of the Jewish people will be cared for in the messianic age. Even the type of basket used is distinctively different from the basket used in the second multiplication story. The basket used in the first story is called, in Greek, a *kophinoy,* a large round basket in which items are carried on the head.

The baskets used to collect the food following the second miracle were different. These baskets, known as *spyridas,* had handles for hand carrying and could never be confused with *kophinoy.* Without a doubt, Mark believed there were two multiplication miracles, and anyone who is serious about the Bible must concede to the possibility of two separate, though similar, miracles.

In the second multiplication story, seven baskets of food are left, no doubt in reference to the seven Gentile nations who had occupied the Land at some point before the Jewish people arrived. Luke records a sermon by Paul in Acts 13:16-41, a portion of which reads:

"You Israelites, and others who fear God, listen. The God of this people Israel chose our ancestors and made the people great during their stay in the land of Egypt, and with uplifted arm he led them out of it. For about forty years he put up with them in the wilderness. After he had destroyed seven nations in the land of Canaan, he gave them their land as an inheritance." (vv. 16-19)[32]

This is Mark's way of stating that not only is there enough food left for the twelve tribes, but that there is enough for the Gentiles as well. This second miracle is directly related to Jesus' second "conversion," during his encounter with the Syrophoenician woman. An early Christian tradition locates the second miracle of multiplication at Tel Hadar (known in the first century as Dodekathronos). This site is found a few kilometers north of Kursi.

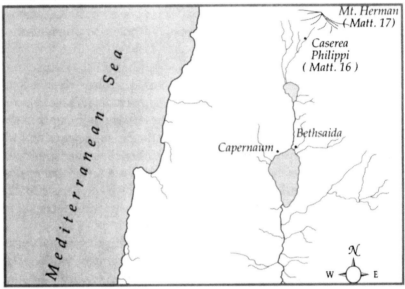

46. *Caesarea Philippi and Mt. Hermon*

From the Decapolis, Jesus traveled to Caesarea Philippi, passing through Bethsaida.[33] He could not return to Capernaum at this time, certainly due to the political trouble caused by the people who wanted to make him king by force. While he was here, Mark reports, he healed a blind man (Mark 8:22-26).

The Conclusion of the Galilean Ministry

As has been suggested above, as Jesus' popularity grew the more Herod Antipas sought him. The events recorded in Mark 4–8 demonstrate that Jesus was constantly on the move, perhaps keeping one step ahead of Herod. Even when he was able to go home to Capernaum, he could not stay long because Herod was trying to capture him and to have him executed, as he had done to John. By the time Jesus returned from his second journey to the Decapolis, things were out of hand and beyond his control. His only choice was to leave the country. In Mark 8, Jesus travels to Gaulinitus, to the region of Caesarea Philippi. It is here that he asked, "Who do people say that I am?" (Mark 8:27), and we have Peter's confession that Jesus is the Messiah.

Following Peter's confession, Jesus revealed to his disciples that he would go to Jerusalem to die. This is the first time that Jesus mentions his own impending death. Up until this time, death, for Jesus, was probably only a philosophical idea and not an impending reality. By this time, he realizes that the socio-political climate in Galilee and the response of the people to his ministry, particularly their response to the first miracle of multiplication, have doomed him. The disciples, who seem to have thought of the messiah as a political/military champion who would reestablish the monarchy and initiate the rule of God, rejected this talk of death. They certainly had no conception of the suffering servant model or atonement theories. Peter reacted to the news of Jesus' impending death by denying its possibility. Jesus verbally reprimanded Peter for his lack of vision and understanding.

Caesarea Philippi was the capital city for Herod Philip and Gaulinitis. A sanctuary to the god Pan, the god of nature, was located here. This is easy to understand since this is a place filled with natural beauty; the Jordan River begins here.[34] Located at Caesarea Philippi was a cave known as the Cave of Pan:

> Josephus, speaking of the Cave of Pan, writes that "hard by the foundations of Jordan . . . there is a top of a mountain that is raised to an immense height, and at its side, beneath, or at its bottom, a dark cave opens; within which is a horrible precipice, that descends abruptly to a vast depth; it contains a mighty quantity of water, which is immovable; and when anybody lets down anything to measure the depth of the earth beneath the water, no length of cord is sufficient to reach it." This cave was known colloquially as the entrance to the underworld or the

"gates of Hades," ("powers of death") (see Matthew 16:18). Jesus literally took his disciples to the "gates of Hades" to ask them "Who do people say that I am?," and for Peter's confession.[35]

47. The Cave of Pan. The mythical entrance to the underworld, located in Caesarea Philippi.

Following the announcement of his imminent death, Jesus taught the disciples for six days. At this time, he took Peter, James, and John, separately, up on a mountain near Caesarea Philippi, "he was transfigured before them, and his clothes became dazzling white, such as no one on earth could bleach them" (Mark 9:2-3). Tradition has located the site of the transfiguration of Jesus at Mt. Tabor, in the Jezreel Valley. However, recent scholarship identifies Mt. Hermon as the mount of the transfiguration, due to its proximity to Caesarea Philippi.

At this point, Jesus' Galilee ministry was essentially over. From Gaulanitis, Jesus and the disciples returned to Capernaum for a brief visit and then were off to Judea and Jerusalem for the final confrontation.

Other Aspects of Jesus' Galilean Ministry

Before leaving Galilee behind, we need to consider a few specific aspects of Jesus' Galilean ministry not mentioned above.

48. Mt. Tabor. The traditional location of the Transfiguration.

An understanding of the Land is critical to the comprehension of some of the teachings, miracles, and parables of Jesus. Let us look at a few specific passages from the New Testament to see how an understanding of the Land, the culture of the times, and prevailing Jewish theological principles may enlighten us.

Earlier we discussed the cultural implications of the offering and receiving of a cup of water. To be offered a drink and then to receive that drink of water was like a social contract in that this act of hospitality would require both the giver and the receiver to be friends for one year. There was also an implied social contract between people who ate together, requiring that they be friends for the rest of their lives. This is what is meant by a "meal covenant." Again, like the giving and receiving of something to drink, this practice continues today among some segments of the peasant classes in the Middle East.[36]

49. Mt. Hermon. The probable location of the Transfiguration.

The parable of the prodigal son provides a New Testament example of such a social contract. In this story, the son asks his father for his inheritance while the father is still living. This act would have been scandalous in the first century, for it would have been a great insult to the father. It was legal for a son to receive his inheritance early, but for him to ask for it would have been perceived as wishing his father were dead.[37] Yet, even if the father divided his property, the son could not sell any of the land. The father would continue to receive a percentage of the produce of the land as a form of social security. Thus the son would need his father's permission to sell the land. Therefore, two legal actions were necessary before the son could convert the property into cash. The Mishnah is quite clear on this issue:

> If a man assigned his goods to his sons he must write, 'From to-day and after my death.' So R. Judah. R. Jose says: He need not do so. If a man assigned his goods to his son to be his after his death, the father cannot sell them since they are assigned to his son, and the son cannot sell them since they are in his father's possession. If his father sold them, they are sold (only) until he dies; if the son sold them, the buyer has no claim on them until the father dies. The father may pluck up (the crop of a field which he has so assigned) and give to eat to whom he will, and if

he left anything already plucked up, it belongs to (all) his heirs. If he left elder sons and younger sons, the elder sons may not care for themselves (out of the common inheritance) at the cost of the younger sons, nor may the younger sons claim maintenance at the cost of the elder sons, but they all share alike.[38]

In the parable the son travels to a "far country."[39] Here, Luke reports, "He squandered his property in loose living," and finally had to find work tending to swine.[40] After he came to his senses, he decided to return to his home and his family. He decided to ask his father to hire him on as a servant.

However, Luke writes: "But while he was still far off, his father saw him and was filled with compassion; he ran and put his arms around him and kissed him" (Luke 15:20). Contemporary Arabs have interpreted the reason why the father runs to meet his son in this manner as meaning that the son will be protected by the father from the other men of the village, who would, under the law, stone the son to death (see Deut. 21:18-21). Yet the father is watching and waiting for his son to return and ready to protect his younger son from the justice of the people of the village.

After the father and son embrace, the father presents his son with four very specific gifts, all of which were symbols of restoration in first- (and twentieth-) century culture. First, the father gives his son a robe. Certainly the younger son needed new clothing. After all, he had been attending to swine, and his clothes were probably torn and tarnished. We might imagine that the father gave to this young son a *tallit*, the prayer shawl that symbolizes the keeping of the covenant. By giving his son his own *tallit*, or prayer shawl, the father symbolically welcomes his son back to the covenant people, to the people of God.

Second, the son is given a ring. This may have been a family signet ring (see above). By making the impression of the family seal on a clay tablet, one could carry out financial and legal transactions. Here the son is restored to the family property and bankroll.

Third, the father orders that his son be given new shoes. In the first century, the only people who went barefoot were slaves and servants. Here it is helpful for us to remember the younger son's well rehearsed speech: "Father, I have sinned against heaven and before you; I am no longer worthy to be called your son; treat me like one of your hired hands" (Luke 15:18-19). By placing shoes on his son's feet, the father demonstrates that his son is not a servant, but a son. This is a symbol of restoration to the family, to sonship.

Finally, the father says, "Get the fatted calf and kill it, and let us eat and celebrate" (Luke 15:23). Kenneth Bailey informs us:

> A rabbinic commentary on Lamentations refers to the people of Jerusalem and notes that none of them would attend a banquet unless he was invited twice (Midrash Rabbah Lam. 4:2, Sonc., 216). . . . Rather the double invitation is in perfect harmony with the traditional Middle Eastern custom, which still persists in conservative areas. A village host must provide meat for a banquet. The meat will be killed and cooked on the basis of the number of guests. A host sends out his invitations and receives acceptance. He then decides on the killing/butchering of a chicken or two (for 2-4 guests), or a duck (for 5-8), or a kid (10-15 acceptances), or a sheep (if there are 15-35 people), or a calf (35-75). That is, the decision regarding the kind of meat and the amount is made mostly on the basis of the number of accepted invitations.[41]

As with the custom whereby the giving and receiving of a drink of water was a social contract of friendship for one year, in the Middle East there is a custom whereby if people eat together they are required by custom to be friends for the rest of their lives. Sharing a meal, or breaking bread together, means lifelong friendship. This is an act, on the part of the father, of saying to his son, "No matter what has happened, I have always been and always will be your friend."

The son is restored to the covenant people (covenant relationship), to the family's financial base, to the family, and, finally, to friendship. The hearers of this parable must have been amazed at the graciousness of the father up to this point in the story. Unfortunately, the story does not end here. We must also consider the older son. For every positive action on the part of the father with regard to the younger son, there is a negative consequence for the older son. First of all, there was a custom in the first century that the older son would inherit the father's *tallit*. Here, the father gives his *tallit* to the younger son. Second, the father restores the younger son to access to the family finances by giving him the signet ring, the father's seal. The younger son has spent all of his inheritance. All that remains is the property of the older son. Now the father is giving away to the younger son property that by law belongs to the older son. Finally, the father orders the killing of the fatted calf, an animal that is customarily killed and cooked for a large wedding banquet. Yet, the father slaughters the animal for a welcome home celebration for the wayward younger son.

When the older son discovers what is happening at home he refuses to participate—and small wonder. He refuses to reestablish the covenant of friendship with his brother. For him the younger brother is dead. For the father, the younger son is literally alive again.

This is a classic example of how we must have some understanding of ancient as well as contemporary culture and custom to better comprehend the message of the Bible, in general, and the New Testament, more specifically.

Understanding the importance of sharing a meal together helps us to better understand other meals mentioned in the New Testament. Jesus shared a meal in the home of Levi (Matthew) the tax collector (Matt. 9:9-13; Mark 2:13-17; Luke 5:27-32), in the multiplication miracles, in the homes of leaders of the Pharisees (Matt. 12:9-14; 26:6-13; Mark 3:1-6; 14:3-9; Luke 7:36-50; 14:1ff.), and in the upper room. In the story of Zacchaeus, for instance, we find that Jesus did not preach to the tax collector. Jesus simply said that he wanted to go home with Zacchaeus for a meal, and the simple offer of friendship prompted Zacchaeus to repent.

In the upper room, Jesus knew that Judas was going to betray him. Judas probably knew that Jesus knew. Yet the unspoken message between Jesus and Judas was one of lifelong friendship.[42]

CHAPTER FOUR

THE JUDEAN MINISTRY

Following their time together at Caesarea Philippi and the reported transfiguration, Jesus and his disciples went to Jerusalem for what would be the last week of Jesus' life. Therefore, we look now to Holy Week for insights into his ministry in Judea and Jerusalem.

A Chronology of Holy Week

The traditional chronology of Holy Week adopted by Christian tradition can be charted as follows:

Sunday	Palm Sunday processional
Monday	Cleansing of the Temple
Tuesday	Teaching in and around the Temple
Wednesday	Private teaching of the disciples
	Jesus in hiding?
Thursday	Private teaching and in hiding
Thursday evening	Last Supper
	Arrest in Gethsemane
	First trial/hearing
	Overnight in house of Caiaphas
Friday	Trial before Sanhedrin
	Trial before Pilate
	Beating
	Execution and death
Easter Sunday	Resurrection

111

There is considerable discussion of a revised chronology of Holy Week from that one traditionally held by the church. This revised chronology accepts the traditional events of the first three days. Some scholars, however, believe that it is possible that the Last Supper took place on Tuesday evening. What are the reasons? First of all, the New Testament does not tell us either the day or the date when the Last Supper occurred. Thus Maundy Thursday is only a tradition of the Church; the New Testament does not say explicitly that Jesus ate this meal with his disciples on Thursday. Second, the New Testament is very explicit about Jesus' activity and movements on Sunday, Monday, and Tuesday, but is very silent about Wednesday and Thursday. Could it be that Jesus had already been arrested and imprisoned on these days? Third, I believe the most compelling argument for an early arrest is that it would be difficult for Jesus to go through all that he experienced from the Last Supper to Gethsemane to the house of Annas to Caiaphas, then overnight in jail, then to the Sanhedrin, to Pilate, to Herod Antipas, back to Pilate, sent to be flogged, returned to Pilate, and then to Calvary in the few hours that would have been available between his arrest on Thursday night to his execution at 9:00 on Friday morning. Those who have been in Jerusalem, who know the lay of the land, realize that this would be highly unlikely, given the distances Jesus would have been required to travel throughout this episode. We must consider the possibility that he was arrested on Tuesday, or, at the very least, at some point before Thursday. In the final analysis, we cannot know for certain the days and dates because we do not know the year of Jesus' death. For the purpose of our discussion here, we will consider that the Last Supper was shared on Tuesday evening.

We should also say a word about the differences in the chronologies among the Gospels. Christian piety has, for the most part, accepted the model offered by the Gospel of Mark. Mark writes that Jesus returned to Bethany at the end of the day on Palm Sunday. "Then he entered Jerusalem and went into the temple; and when he had looked around at everything, as it was already late, he went out to Bethany with the twelve" (Mark 11:11).

Matthew and Luke report the attack on the money changers as taking place on Palm Sunday. "Then Jesus entered the temple and drove out all who were selling and buying in the temple, and he overturned the tables of the money changers and the seats of those who sold doves. He said to them, 'It is written, "My house shall be called a house of prayer"; but you are making it a den of robbers' " (Matt. 21:12-13). John places the attack against the money changers very early, during the period of preparation before the arrest of John the Baptist (John 2:13-22). I will here be using the traditional chronology, considering the cleansing of the Temple to have occurred on Monday, even though we cannot know with any certainty when, or if, it happened on this day.

Palm Sunday

According to the Gospel accounts, Jesus traveled from Caesarea Philippi/Mt. Hermon in the north to Jerusalem. It is reported that he passed through Perea on his trip to the south: "He left that place and went to the region of Judea and beyond the Jordan. And crowds again gathered around him; and, as was his custom, he again taught them" (Mark 10:1; see also Matt. 19:1ff.). An adult in good health could travel about twenty miles (thirty-six kilometers) in one day. Allowing for stops along the way (see Luke's account), we may suppose that Jesus and the disciples traveled about two weeks on their journey from the north to Jerusalem. They traveled through the Jordan Valley, Jericho, the Wadi Qelt,[1] and on to Bethany.

Along the way, the Gospel writers report, Jesus taught and healed people. Interestingly, both Matthew and Mark report that some Pharisees came to him and asked about divorce. Although it is generally agreed that Jesus' teaching was rooted in first-century CE Hillelian theology, on this issue Jesus appeared to agree more with the House of Shammai:

> Jesus also opposed any excessive hairsplitting, and preferred to uphold the moral point of view. In matters of divorce, for example, he was as stringent as the School of Shammai (so in

113

Matthew 5:32; 19:3-9). From unpublished research by Professor Shmuel Safrai it appears that in this matter the School of Shamai took the more stringent view because of its special consideration for the woman. The attitude of the School of Hillel was more liberal-but only toward the man. The School of Shammai looked after the woman's interest in other cases as well.

According to Matthew, Jesus adopted the point of view of the School of Shammai in order to justify the indissolubility of marriage in the case of fornication. On the same point, the position of the Essenes, who did not permit marriages to be dissolved in any case, was later incorporated into the New Testament-but that was already under the influence of Paul, who directly related to the Essenes.

Here Jesus accepted the position of the School of Shammai as a matter of practical Jewish Law and not for theocentric reasons which were typical of that School. In his attitude to people, on the other hand, he was closer to the School of Hillel, and the love of man was central to his teaching. His acceptance of the more stringent rulings of the School of Shammai had its origins in his fear of sin and his desire that man should live in an atmosphere of perfect holiness.[2]

The Synoptic Gospels inform us that Jesus was heavily involved in teaching along the way. When he reached Jericho, Luke reports, Jesus' encountered Zacchaeus, the tax collector. Eventually, Jesus made his way to Bethany and Bethphage. One of the more difficult hikes in Israel today is the climb from Bethany to Bethphage and then on over the Mount of Olives to Jerusalem's Old City. Certainly this would also have been true in the first century CE. The climb is almost straight up and requires the traveler to be in excellent condition. Jesus and the disciples came to Bethany, after walking from Caesarea Philippi in the north, and then hiked to Bethphage; Jesus rode on a donkey only the last half mile to Jerusalem. Why would Jesus have walked all that great distance and then have ridden this short distance to Jerusalem?

The Bible tells us that we will know when the Messiah comes because he will be riding on a donkey: "Rejoice greatly, O daughter Zion! Shout aloud, O daughter Jerusalem! Lo, your king comes to you; triumphant and victorious is he, humble and riding on a donkey, on a colt, the foal of a donkey" (Zech. 9:9). However, the Bible does not tell from whence the Messiah will ride this donkey or when. For first-century rabbis, these questions were very important. They did not want to miss the coming of the Messiah, so they debated the location from which the Messiah would ride the donkey into Jerusalem. They knew they could not determine when he would come, but it might be possible for them to locate the direction he would enter the city.

Thus rabbinical tradition determined that the Messiah would ride into Jerusalem from the city limits on the eastern side of the city. The Mishnah states that the city limits on the eastern side of the city were found in the small village of Bethphage. "It is in doubt whether the wall of the City or the wall of the Temple Court is intended. R. Johanan (*Gem.* 75b) explains it as 'the wall of Bethphage.' Bethphage marked the limit of the confines of Jerusalem" (*Mishnah Menahoth* 7:3n).[3]

50. *Palm Sunday Church at Bethphage. The traditional site of the beginning of the Palm Sunday procesion.*

Jesus' riding on a donkey had messianic implications beyond the prophecy. In 1 Kings, David discusses the anointing of Solomon as his successor: " 'Summon to me the priest Zadok, the prophet Nathan, and Benaiah son of Jehoiada.' When they came before the king, the king said to them, 'Take with you the servants of your lord, and have my son Solomon ride on my own mule, and bring him down to Gihon. There let the priest Zadok and the prophet Nathan anoint him king over Israel.' " (1 Kings 1:32-34).[4] Thus Jesus' riding into Jerusalem on a donkey (or mule) suggested that he was a part of the Davidic dynasty to the public.

By walking from the Galilee to Bethphage and then mounting the donkey, Jesus was intentionally bringing together the biblical prophecy of Zechariah and the rabbinic interpretation. He was, in fact, saying "I am the Messiah" without saying a word. All of the people in the area also knew the prophecy and interpretation, and they greeted Jesus with shouts of "Hosanna," waving palm branches and other cut branches and spreading their garments on the road in front of him as he passed by. All of these actions or reactions by the crowd spoke to their understanding of Jesus' silent message.

51. *The Palm Sunday Route. The modern village of Bethphage along the Palm Sunday route.*

116

52. *The Church of St. Mary Magdalene. A portion of the first-century Roman road is preserved here.*

53. *Church of Dominus Flevit. This
church preserves the tradition of
Jesus' weeping over Jerusalem on
Palm Sunday (Luke 19:41-44).*

The custom of spreading one's outer garments in the path was reserved for royalty. Thus the people were creating a royal procession for Jesus and his disciples. By shouting "Hosanna" (meaning literally "Save us"), the crowd was calling out to Jesus to save them—not from their sins, but from the Romans. In waving palm branches they were fanning the flames of Jewish nationalism. The palm branch was a symbol of the Hasmonean Monarchy and the Maccabean Revolt in the 160s BCE, and thereby a symbol of Jewish nationalism in the first century.[5] The people wanted Jesus to do to the Romans what Judah the Hammer had done to the Greeks in 164 BCE.[6]

With all of the excitement, a large crowd gathered and followed Jesus and the processional across the Mount of Olives to Jerusalem. A portion of the old Roman road is preserved today in a part of the Garden of Gethsemane, located on the property of the Church of St. Mary Magdalene.

Luke's Gospel reports that as Jesus descended the Mount of Olives to the Temple Mount, he wept over the city. "If you, even you, had only recognized on this day the things that make for peace! But now they are hidden from your eyes. Indeed, the days will come upon you, when your enemies will set up ramparts around you and surround you, and hem you in on every side. They will crush you to the ground, you and your children within you, and they will not leave within you one stone upon another; because you did not recognize the time of your visitation from God." (Luke 19:42-44). This act of weeping is remembered today in the Church of Dominus Flevit (the church where "the Lord wept").[7]

As soon as they crossed the Mount of Olives they would come into view of the Antonia Fortress, the Roman military headquarters in Jerusalem, where the soldiers standing guard on the towers would have noticed the procession. We may speculate that the Romans, very effective in their ability to occupy and dominate subjugated peoples and nations, would have known of the prophecy of Zechariah, the rabbinic interpretation, palm branches, donkey rides from Bethphage, and the meaning of the word *hosanna*. Immediately the Roman soldiers would have called this procession to the attention of their superiors. Jewish religious leaders also would have been aware of the danger this kind of demonstration might pose, and thus they asked Jesus to silence the crowd (Luke 19:40). Jesus responded by telling the Jewish religious leaders that an announcement was being made. They should join in the celebration rather than try to quiet the crowd (Luke 19:39-40).

Theoretically, the Romans' first exposure to Jesus of Nazareth might have occurred on Palm Sunday. There was no reason for the Romans to have heard of him before this time. Jesus lived in

54. The Antonia Fortress. This was the Roman military headquarters in Jerusalem. Soldiers standing quard on the towers would have witnessed the Palm Sunday parade over the Mt. of Olives.

Capernaum in Galilee, and he was the subject of Herod Antipas. The only Roman to have been exposed to Jesus, his teaching, his popularity, was the centurion who lived in Capernaum, and he was either a Jewish sympathizer or a convert to the Jewish faith.[8] Jesus was popular in Galilee, and it was there that people wanted to make him king by force. Pontius Pilate, the Roman Procurator of Judea (from 26 to 36 CE), lived in Caesarea Maritima and came to Jerusalem only on special occasions, a few times a year. There would have been no reason for him to have known of Jesus. Jesus was Herod's problem. Therefore, the Romans would have been caught by surprise by this spontaneous reaction to a young rabbi riding into the Holy City on a donkey from Bethphage, the city limits. On Palm Sunday, the Roman army went on alert in Jerusalem, and Rome was awakened to the potential danger of Jesus. The officers of the Antonia Fortress certainly took action to find out who this man was and why the people were so excited by him.

There was another group in town who might also have been energized by this Palm Sunday procession. The Zealots were looking for a charismatic figure to help them rally the people to revolt against Rome. Witnessing the Palm Sunday parade must have stimulated their hopes. Seeing Jesus received as he was by the masses, they might have come to the conclusion that the time for action was at hand.

What we see happening here is that two groups of political enemies are awakened and energized on Palm Sunday. The Romans realized that they had to act to keep a dangerous situation from getting out of hand. The Zealots realized that they might have found a charismatic leader to be the cornerstone of their insurrection against Roman rule in Palestine, and they too should act, if the opportunity presented itself. The Zealots were the one force united and dedicated to removing the Romans from the land:

> The rise of the Fourth Philosophy underscores the blurred line that separated the religious/nonpolitical realm from the religious/political realm. From the point of view of the founders of the Fourth Philosophy (the Zealots), the call for revolution against Rome was inspired by religious, not political zeal. They claimed that it was blasphemous to call any individual *despotes*, lord, master, emperor. God and God alone was *despotes*, Lord, Master, Emperor. . . . The fact that Judas and Zadok (founders of the movements) were sages, not soldiers, and the fact that Josephus dignified this revolutionary movement by setting it beside the schools of thought of the Sadducees, Pharisees, and Essenes as another religious philosophy within Judaism attest to the religious wellspring of this violent challenge to Rome.[9]

The people of Judea, and also Galilee and Peraea, hated the Romans for their repressive rule. Many of the common people who did not possess their religious zeal nevertheless supported their efforts and hoped that one day the Romans would be driven out. Certainly the Zealots saw in Jesus a potential ally, or at the least a popular and charismatic figure around whom they could unite the masses in their revolt against Rome, a revolt in which God would be on their side.

The Romans were as determined to keep the peace and to control the masses as were the Zealots to disrupt the peace and inspire the masses to revolt. Judea had been a cacophony of political unrest since the days just prior to the death of Herod the Great. The situation was so volatile that Rome had instituted direct rule by replacing Herod Archelaus, who had succeeded his father as ruler in Judea, with a series of Roman procurators. Pontius Pilate, who ruled Judea for Rome, had come to Palestine in 26 CE. Rivkin informs us:

> When Pontius Pilate entered on his procuratorship in AD 26 and immediately reconfirmed Caiaphas as high priest, he fell heir to a country that had been wracked by continuous violence . . . Judea was clearly no sinecure. It was, rather, a battleground where the mettle of the procurator and his high priest was put to the test day-in and day-out. If Pontius Pilate were to make his mark and show himself worthy of advancement in the hierarchy of imperial power, it was essential that he impress the emperor with his ability to maintain law and order in a land which had proven itself to be a seedbed of dissidence, disorder, and violence. Tiberias (AD 14–37), who had succeeded Augustus as emperor and had appointed Pilate, was scarcely in the mood for a repetition of the years of turbulence that had shaken Judea after the death of Herod. Unless, then, Pontius Pilate were shrewd enough to govern this unruly people, his tenure as procurator was bound to be extremely short.[10]

Jesus found himself caught between these two diametrically opposed forces, which were moving toward a point of confrontation and climax. Palm Sunday was critical for Jesus, and the events of that day aroused Rome against Jesus and the Zealots to support him as someone around whom they could rally the people. Mark's Gospel informs us that at the end of the processional, Jesus entered the Temple, took a look around at what was going on, and withdrew to Bethany for the night. On Monday, Jesus returned to Jerusalem via the road between

55. *Robinson's Arch. This marks the location of the monumental staircase that served as the southwestern entrance into the Court of the Gentiles, the primary entrance for the poor from the Lower City.*

Bethany and Bethphage. While passing along, perhaps as he-passed Bethphage, he cursed a fig tree. They proceeded on to the Temple, at which he performed the "cleansing." We must ask ourselves why Jesus would attack the money changers as he did. But before we hazard a guess, let us consider who were these people changing money and selling pigeons.

The Cleansing of the Temple

The money changers carried out a legal, necessary, and important function for sacrificial worship in the Temple. Many of the laws found in the Torah require that animals be offered at various occasions as sacrifices for sin, purification, and so forth or as offerings for such events as the birth of a child. Furthermore, it was a custom of the day that no pagan money—that is, money bearing images, a practice considered as idolatrous— could be used in the Temple or its precincts. People who did not have Jewish currency would be required to change "pagan" money before they entered into the Court of the Gentiles. The money changers were located just inside the entrance gate in the southwestern corner of the Temple Mount, in an area just

56. Model of the Temple Mount, Showing the Place of the Money Changers

57. Model of the Primary Entrance to the Temple Mount

beyond what is known today as Robinson's Arch, which was in the first century CE the primary entrance for those living in the Lower City.

Why did Jesus carry out this attack against the money changers? Probably because the level of corruption involving the various people who received a profit or commission or a kick-back from the sale of animals and the changing of money had made it practically impossible for the poor to carry out the sacrifices required by the Law. So many commissions were built in to the price of animals used in sacrifices that the cost had become prohibitive for the poor. Thus the Temple and its sacrificial worship had become inaccessible to the poor! God's house could no longer be thought of as a "house of prayer." Literally and figuratively the Temple had become a den of robbers, and the chief robber was the high priest!

It is important to remember that the Sadducees controlled the Temple and any business conducted there. They certainly received either a commission on or profit from the items sold or the money exchanged there. Furthermore, they were the party of the wealthy, the aristocracy. Josephus emphasizes this point: "The Sadducees are able to persuade none but the rich, and have not the populace obsequious to them, but the Pharisees have the multitude on their side."[11] They also held the power to administer civil law on behalf of the Romans. We must not forget that Pilate, and all of the Roman procurators, lived in Caesarea Maritima. The high priest and his associates controlled Jerusalem and the Temple. Rivkin adds these considerations:

> The Roman imperial framework, within which Jesus' life, preaching, trial, crucifixion, and attested resurrection took place, is clear enough. At the pinnacle of power and authority was the emperor, who exercised his authority over the Jews either through puppet kings, like Herod, or through procurators, like Coponius and Pontius Pilate. These imperial instruments, in turn, sought to carry out their responsibilities to the emperor by appointing high priests, who were selected for their pliancy rather than their piety. Their function was to serve as the eyes and ears of the puppet king or procurator, so as to head off demonstrative challenges to Roman rule. Of these high priests, only one—Caiaphas—had such piercing eyes and such keen ears that he was able to keep the confidence of the procurators he served as long as he remained in office.
>
> But even Caiaphas could scarcely have done his job single-handedly. It is thus highly likely that he appointed a council, or sanhedrin, consisting of individuals who were well aware of the dire consequences that would follow any outbreak against Roman authority, however innocent and naive its instigator. To

124

be sure, such a sanhedrin is not specifically mentioned by Josephus in his account of the incumbency of Pontius Pilate and Caiaphas. But he does mention such a sanhedrin when he tells us of the trial and stoning of James, the brother of Jesus. . . .

Josephus' account of the stoning of James is of vital importance, for it reveals the role of the high priest as being that of the procurator's procurator. It also reveals the thin line that separated the religious from the political realm.[12]

The Sadducees controlled the Temple and civil law for the Romans. When Jesus attacked the money changers he was indirectly attacking Rome, an act of sedition. Not only was Jesus creating political problems for the Sadducees by attacking the Temple, but also he was obstructing the Sadducees' business and profits.

As already stated, it is likely that the Romans had not heard of Jesus or, at least, considered him no more of a threat than any other political agitator—until Palm Sunday. The Sadducees probably had not paid much attention to Jesus either. They were a local Jerusalem sect, and Jesus, the Galilean, would have been much more familiar to the Pharisees and Essenes. However, after Jesus' attack on the Temple and the money changers, the Sadducees would have been forced to silence this threat to their power and to the peace of Jerusalem. On Monday, they, like the Romans on Sunday, would decide that Jesus must be removed from the scene before he could do any more damage. John reports a meeting of some of the religious leaders:

"What are we to do? This man is performing many signs. If we let him go on like this, everyone will believe in him, and the Romans will come and destroy both our holy place and our nation." But one of them, Caiaphas, who was high priest that year, said to them, "You know nothing at all! You do not understand that it is better for you to have one man die for the people than to have the whole nation destroyed." (John 11:47-50)

Think of how the Zealots might have reacted to the attack on the Temple. If they were energized by the Palm Sunday parade and the popularity of Jesus, they would have been overwhelmed by Jesus' actions on Monday. Perhaps they were even making plans for the revolution to begin, getting organized silently behind the scenes. By this time they might have been waiting for just the right moment. On Tuesday, however, Jesus, who had now alienated both the Romans and the Sadducees, would alienate the Zealots as well.

Teaching in the Temple

After the attack on the Temple, Jesus left the city and returned to Bethany. The following morning he and his disciples returned again to Jerusalem, where they passed by the place where

58. The Herodion—Exterior

Jesus had cursed a fig tree the day before. The disciples asked him about this, and Jesus said, "Have faith in God. Truly I tell you, if you say to this mountain, 'Be taken up and thrown into the sea,' and if you do not doubt in your heart, but believe that what you say will come to pass, it will be done for you" (Mark 11:22-23). If a person has enough faith, he or she will be able to move mountains.

Jesus was possibly passing along from Bethphage to the Mount of Olives when this teaching was offered. From the road along which they traveled one can see off on the horizon to the south the mountain fortress of the Herodion, Herod the Great's summer palace, some seven miles (eleven kilometers) south of Jerusalem. The Herodion Fortress is built inside an artificial mountain that resembles a volcanic cone. To create this struc-ture, Herod the Great had the dirt removed from one hill and piled up on another. It was hollow on the inside, and a very tall

59. The Herodion—Interior. The Herodion served as Herod's summer palace. Josephus reports that Herod the Great was buried here as well. The Herodian was also used by the Zealots during the Second Jewish Revolt (132-135).

fortification wall surrounded its perimeter. This was a mountain that was literally moved!

Furthermore, from the Mount of Olives, on a clear day, the Dead Sea is visible to the southeast. In the West we often misinterpret Jesus' meaning when he says we may move mountains, believing that he is talking about magic or, perhaps, telekinesis. Yet, this is a very practical teaching, conforming to pragmatic Hillelian thought: "You can do unbelievable things if you are

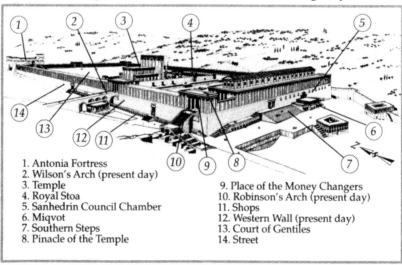

1. Antonia Fortress
2. Wilson's Arch (present day)
3. Temple
4. Royal Stoa
5. Sanhedrin Council Chamber
6. Miqvot
7. Southern Steps
8. Pinacle of the Temple
9. Place of the Money Changers
10. Robinson's Arch (present day)
11. Shops
12. Western Wall (present day)
13. Court of Gentiles
14. Street

60. The Court of the Gentiles. This was the large area surrounding the Temple where rabbis would teach publicly.

willing to work." You can move mountains, but you must have faith to put a shovel into the ground and bend your back!

From Bethphage, Jesus returned to the Temple, where he would again teach. In the first century, when a rabbi wanted to teach in public he would go to the Temple Mount, in the Court of the Gentiles. Public teaching took place in the colonnade that surrounded the interior walls.[13] Thus when we read that Jesus was teaching "in the temple," this does not mean that he taught in the sanctuary, in the Temple proper, but in the colonnade surrounding the Court of the Gentiles. The style of teaching was not so much sermonic, but rather would have been a series of questions and answers, much like a modern-day *yeshiva*. Very often, in this setting, questions would be answered with questions. Mark reports:

Again they came to Jerusalem. As he was walking in the temple, the chief priests, the scribes, and the elders came to him and said, "By what authority are you doing these things? Who gave you this authority to do them?" Jesus said to them. "I will ask you one question; answer me, and I will tell you by what authority I do these things." (Mark 11:27-29)

While he was teaching here on Tuesday, morning a man came to Jesus and asked, "'Which commandment is the first of all?'

61. *Model of the Court of the Gentiles. Gentiles were allows to enter this court area, but not to go beyond the "Beautiful Gate," which led into the Court of the Women.*

Jesus answered, 'Hear, O Israel: The Lord our God, the Lord is one; and you shall love the Lord your God with all your heart, and with all your soul, and with all your mind, and with all your strength.' The second is this, 'You shall love your neighbor as yourself.' There is no other commandment greater than these' " (Mark 12:28-31). Jesus answered with the classic Hillelian response. The Shema[14] was the central theological concept for Hillelian thought in the first century CE (and continues to be so with theological descendants of the disciples of Hillel). Jesus, in answering as he did, reinforced our theory that he had attached himself to the House of Hillel when he moved to Capernaum.

Various other familiar teachings of Jesus are reported to have taken place on Tuesday morning while he taught on the Temple Mount. Among these are the parable of the vineyard, Jesus' discussion with the Sadducees concerning divorce and the resurrection, and the encounter with some Pharisees and Herodians concerning the issue of paying taxes to Rome, an encounter that would lead to further erosion of Jesus' support base and popularity in Jerusalem.

The Pharisees and Herodians came to Jesus and asked, "Is it lawful to pay taxes to the emperor, or not?" (Mark 12:14). Jesus' reply lets us know that these people did not come to the Temple for worship but for treachery. The fact that they came to Jesus with a coin bearing the image of Caesar—a coin forbidden to be used at the Temple—shows us that they were not there for worship, but to trap Jesus. They were hoping to lure Jesus into making a seditious statement against Rome so that they could have him arrested. Jesus responded by saying:

"Why are you putting me to the test? Bring me a denarius and let me see it." And they brought one. Then he said to them, "Whose head is this and whose title?" They answered, "The emperor's." Jesus said to them, "Give to the emperor the things that are the emperor's, and to God the things that are God's." And they were utterly amazed at him. (Mark 12:15-17)

Luke goes on to add:

And "they were not able in the presence of the people to trap him by what he said; and being amazed by his answer, they became silent." (Luke 20:26)

We have all marveled at how easily Jesus, according to these Gospel accounts, eluded those sent to trap him. However, I would like to suggest that he does not get away so easily. Certainly the Pharisees and Herodians who came to catch him went away unhappy, even though they were amazed at his ability to deflect their devious efforts. But we must consider how the Zealots might have received his response. To be sure, they would have been hanging around in the colonnade, listening to his teaching. They would have been thrilled at the question being raised, because this would have given Jesus the opportunity to validate their own political/religious beliefs about Roman occupation and Rome's right to tax the people (which the Zealots considered as an offering to a pagan and false god).

Imagine their surprise when Jesus said that paying taxes to Rome was a legitimate act. Without a doubt they would have rejected Jesus as a possible leader for their hoped-for revolution. Jesus might even have been labeled a Roman collaborator. Thus in answering as he did, Jesus alienated the Zealots who would have looked to another charismatic leader to further their own political/religious agenda.

This is Tuesday! Already the great crowd who sang "Hosanna!" on Sunday is falling away, little by little. By Tuesday

62. *The Teaching Steps. These steps led to the gates located in the southern walls of the Temple Mount.*

morning Jesus had managed to alienate the Romans, the Sadducees, and the Zealots. There was only one more major power broker remaining, the Pharisees, and they turned away from Jesus, perhaps, on Tuesday afternoon.

The Alienation of the Pharisees

Mark and Luke offer much shorter versions of the conflict reported in Matthew 23. Certainly there is considerable redaction in Matthew's version. Yet, all of the synoptic accounts report that Jesus severely criticized the scribes (and Pharisees) for their failure to properly serve the people. This teaching is set on the steps leading to the entrance at the southern end of the Temple Mount.[15] There are three reasons for locating Jesus' teaching here. First of all, Jesus taught in monologue form (a sermon). These steps were customarily used by rabbis as a place where they could teach their disciples and closest followers privately. Remember, public teaching (through questions and dialogue) took place in the Court of the Gentiles. Here Jesus was delivering a monologue or a sermon. This is clearly private teaching and would have taken place on the steps rather than in the Court of the Gentiles.

Second, the general offices for the Pharisees were located just inside the southern walls. This is also where the Sanhedrin law court was located. Jesus had two audiences: (1) his followers on the steps and (2) the Pharisees inside the southern wall. Here Jesus told his followers how they should live and act by pointing out the hypocrisy of the Pharisees.[16] His pronouncement against them would have been particularly upsetting.

A third reason for placing Jesus' teaching on these steps when he criticized the scribes (and Pharisees) has to do with one of the woes reported by Matthew: "Woe to you, scribes and Pharisees, hypocrites! For you are like whitewashed tombs, which on the outside look beautiful, but inside they are full of the bones of the dead and of all kinds of filth. So you also on the outside look righteous to others, but inside you are full of hypocrisy and lawlessness" (Matt. 23:27-28). Across the Kidron

Valley, in full view of people standing or walking on these steps, is one of the oldest and most important Jewish cemeteries in Israel.[17] Jesus could have been referring to these tombs as his example in the story.

63. Cemetery on the Mount of Olives. Some Jewish traditions state that people buried here will be the first to rise in the resurrection when the Messiah comes. Jesus may have been referring to this cemetery in Matt. 23:27.

Jesus' Third "Conversion" Experience

Matthew 23:37-39 is Jesus' final break with the Pharisees and his final "conversion" experience. On the teaching steps he rejected the Pharisees for their failure to adequately represent the kingdom of God to the people. This passage from Matthew is Jesus' lament over the Pharisees' failure and, perhaps, his own impending doom. He was broken, and he soulfully poured out his heart on these steps: "Jerusalem, Jerusalem, the city that kills the prophets and stones those who are sent to it! How often have I desired to gather your children together as a hen gathers her brood under her wings, and you were not willing! See, your house is left to you, desolate. For I tell you, you will not see me again until you say, 'Blessed is the one who comes in the name of the Lord.' " (Matt. 23:37-39).

Jesus' ministry ended here on these steps. Once the Pharisees turned on him, Jesus was utterly alone against the invincible power brokers of Jerusalem: Romans, Sadducees, Zealots, and Pharisees. He is now a hunted man and must remain in hiding until his eventual capture, arrest, and incarceration.

We may have wondered about how the crowd who sang "Hosanna" on Sunday could turn so quickly and shout "Crucify!" on Friday. I would like to suggest that this crowd had completely reversed itself by Tuesday afternoon. By Tuesday the four principal power groups in Jerusalem had turned against Jesus and had disowned him to their constituencies. Turning the crowd would have been relatively easy.[18] All that was required was simply putting out the word "Jesus has to go." In less than forty-eight hours, Jesus had been transformed from a conquering hero, entering Jerusalem triumphantly on Palm Sunday, to an outcast whose last hours of freedom were lived in the shadows.

Jesus' first "conversion" moved him from the rigid fundamentalism of the Natzoreans, from exclusive Judaism, to the inclusive pluralistic liberalism of the Pharisees of the House of Hillel. After encountering a Gentile woman in the region of Tyre and Sidon, his second "conversion" was a shift from inclusive Judaism to an acceptance of the Gentiles. This was manifested by his second journey to the Decapolis, where his teaching on the kingdom of God and his ministry were extended to the Gentiles. Finally, he broke with the Pharisees and was left alone in hiding with only his closest friends. Now where could he go? With whom could he have associated? Perhaps the Essenes.

Perhaps Jesus was in hiding on Wednesday and Thursday. Perhaps he was arrested on Tuesday night or early Wednesday morning. As stated above, we cannot know for certain when these events took place. The Synoptics report that he taught the disciples in private and shared a final meal with friends in Bethany, perhaps on Monday night (see Mark 14:3-9). The following day he sent Peter and John into Jerusalem with these instructions, " 'Go into the city, and a man carrying a jar of water will meet you; follow him, and wherever he enters, say to the owner of the house, 'The Teacher says, Where is my guest room, where I may eat the Passover with my disciples?' " (Mark 14:13-14; cf. Luke 22:10ff.). Mark and Luke might be giving us a clue to where Jesus and his followers ate the Last Supper.

133

64. The Traditional Site of the Upper Room

The Last Supper

During the first century it was not forbidden for men to carry water. However, Middle Eastern peasant culture would have frowned on such behavior.[19] Water was drawn and brought to the home usually in the early morning or late afternoon. Those who were allowed to bring water to the home, in order of priority, were wives, daughters, male sons under the age of twelve, animals, and, finally, men. If none of the others were available, men could go and bring water. However, due to the cultural stigma associated with this behavior, men would probably never have carried water in public—with one exception.

Celibate monks living a cloistered life would not have had women available to carry water for them, so it would have been acceptable for them to carry water in public without any criticism. Perhaps Jesus had arranged for the Last Supper to be eaten in an Essene monastery and had sent his two disciples there to make

65. *Model of an Essene Monastery. The Last Supper might have taken place in an Essene monastery, which would have been located in this general area of Jerusalem from the Second Temple period.*

the final arrangements.[20] With the Pharisees, Sadducees, and Zealots turned against him, there would be no other place for him go or group to which he could turn. Furthermore, the Essenes might have thought that if the Pharisees and Sadducees were against Jesus, he might be doing something right, and they would have welcomed him. We must also remember that the Natzorean clan/sect was Hasidic in behavior and theology, and Jesus would have fit in there quite well.

Modern scholarship has given us a much better understanding of the Last Supper. This meal would have been a reclining meal eaten at a *triclinium* table,[21] which was most often used by wealthy persons. Archaeology and historical sources have confirmed this at Zippori, the Herodion, and Masada, among other places. During the first century there was a custom that suggested that all people should eat the Passover as a reclining meal, because God had made all Jews wealthy when they were delivered from slavery to freedom during the exodus from Egypt. Furthermore, the Gospel of John is quite explicit in demonstrating that this is a *triclinium* meal: "After saying this Jesus was troubled in spirit, and declared, "Very truly, I tell you, one of you will betray me." The disciples looked at one another, uncertain of whom he was speaking. One of his disciples—the one whom Jesus loved—was reclining next to him" (John 13:21-23).

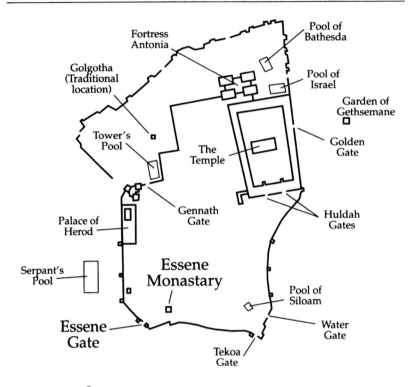

66. *Site of an Essene Monastery*

67. Zippori *triclinium*

136

At a *triclinium* table, seats were specially arranged so that VIP seating was on the left-hand side, as an observer would face the table. Moving to the right, the seats were arranged in a descending order of importance. The last place to the right, in the right-hand corner, was the place of least importance. The person sitting here usually had the responsibility of washing the feet of the guests at a formal meal.[22]

The host would always occupy position two at the table. The attendant would sit, or recline, in position one. The guest of honor was always placed at position three. Knowing this, we can locate at least three people at the Last Supper.

Jesus, the host, would have been sitting, or reclining, in position two. Robert Morgan points out that this was the only meal reported in the New Testament where Jesus was the host: "Unlike other meals where Jesus is a guest, the Last Supper was hosted by Jesus himself."[23] The attendant to the meal, the one who would refill the wine glasses or pitchers, bread plates, and the like, would be placed on the host's right, the one who would be "reclining next to him [the host]" (John 13:23). This person is not identified by name, but only as the "one whom Jesus loved."[24] The guest of honor, the person in the third position, would have been to the host's left, or to the back of the host. In order to speak to the host, John, the attendant, would have had to lay his head back against the breast of Jesus. To speak to the guest of honor, Jesus would have had to lay his head against the breast of the guest of honor—Judas. How do we know that Judas was in this position? All of the Gospel writers agree that Judas, the betrayer, was the one who was either dipping with Jesus (Synoptic Gospels) or the recipient of the sop.[25] The only persons who could share common eating vessels with the host were those to his right and left, the attendant and the guest of honor. Since the attendant, John, asked who would betray Jesus and since Jesus indicates that it was the other person sitting next to him, this could only have been Judas.

We do not know which disciples or followers of Jesus would have occupied the other places, with the possible exception of the last position. It is probable that Peter was here. Three reasons support this theory. First of all, when Jesus announced that one of the disciples would betray him, Peter asked John to ask

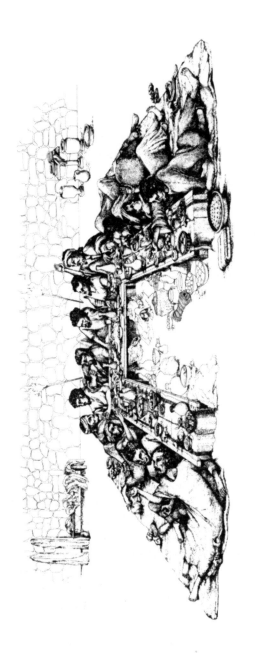

68. *Fleming's Drawing of the Last Supper Seating Arrangement. The Last Supper was lilely a triclinium meal such as this.*

Jesus who it was (see John 13:24). If Peter had been close enough, he could have asked Jesus himself. Second, Peter and John would have been sitting (reclining) directly across from each other. From these positions it would have been easy for these two to communicate. Third, the person in the last position was responsible for the washing of the feet of the guests. John 13 points out that Jesus made this an issue when Peter failed to carry out his responsibility.

Earlier we discussed the social contract initiated through the sharing of a meal. This is a contract of lifelong friendship. Perhaps Jesus was sending to Judas an unspoken message. Not only would Judas be his friend forever, but also he would always have a place of honor within the close circle of friends.

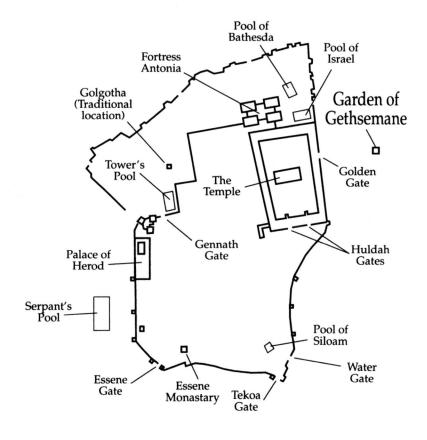

69. *The Old City, Temple Mount, Garden of Gethsemane*

Gethsemane

The Gospels report that Jesus and the disciples went from the upper room to the Garden of Gethsemane, located in the Kiddron Valley east of the walls of the city and the Temple.

An old tradition contends that Jesus came to the garden with the remaining eleven disciples, left eight in a cave (known today as the Cave of the Gethsemane, or colloquially as the Cave of the Betrayal), then went on with three disciples to pray. The Synoptic accounts all agree with this and are certainly the inspiration for the Christian tradition surrounding this cave.

> They went to a place called Gethsemane; and he said to his disciples (the eight), "Sit here while I pray." He took with him Peter and James and John, and began to be distressed and agitated. And he said to them, "I am deeply grieved, even to death; remain here, and keep awake." (Mark 14:32-34)

Mark goes on to report (as do Matthew and Luke) that Jesus tried to pray, but his distress would not allow him to concentrate. The picture drawn by the Synoptic writers is that of a very nervous Jesus, waiting for the soldiers to come for him. This is perfectly

70. The Church of All Nations. This church was built over the traditional place where Jesus prayed in the Garden of Gethsemane.

140

understandable. Anyone facing imminent arrest, torture, and execution would not be able to concentrate or focus on prayer. When he returned to his friends, he found them asleep. In great anguish, he asked them to stay awake and to watch for him, but to no avail. He moved from his place of solitude to his three sleeping friends, back and forth, two more times with no luck. He was not able to pray, and they were not able to stay awake. In Luke's version we are told that when Jesus prayed he was in so much agony that his perspiration was like drops of blood falling from his head.[26]

Christian piety also suggests that when Jesus prayed he knelt beside a rock that is located today under the Basilica of the Agony.[27] The church is built in a garden that contains some very old olive trees. The modern Garden of Gethsemane, which surrounds the church, is only a small portion of the olive grove located here during the first century.

After Jesus failed in his efforts to pray, soldiers came and arrested him in the Garden of Gethsemane. His friends all abandoned him, running away in fear, and Jesus was led away to the house of the high priest.

71. Olive Trees from Gethsemane

Trial Before the Jewish Leadership

The Gospel of John reports that Jesus was first taken to the house of Annas[28] and then on to the house of Caiaphas. In John's Gospel, Annas is referred to as the high priest (18:22). Stern explains how Annas bore the title: "The period [Second Temple] was marked by rapid, successive changes in the office of

141

high priest. This situation naturally accounts for the presence of a certain number of former high priests who continued to bear the title even if they no longer held the office."[29] The same principle applies to living former presidents in the United States. The fact that Jesus was questioned first by Annas suggests that Annas likely continued to hold significant power—perhaps even more than Caiaphas himself.

When Jesus was questioned by Annas, he offered the most frank and straightforward defense he would offer on his own behalf. John writes:

> Then the high priest questioned Jesus about his disciples and about his teaching. Jesus answered, "I have spoken openly to the world; I have always taught in synagogues and in the temple, where all the Jews come together. I have said nothing in secret. Why do you ask me? Ask those who heard what I said to them; they know what I said." (John 18:19-21)

Following this brief encounter, Annas sent Jesus to Caiaphas.

72. St. Peter's in Gallicantu. The traditional location of the house of Caiaphas and the trial of Jesus.

Jesus was brought to the house of Caiaphas in the Upper City of Jerusalem. The house of the high priest functioned much as the White House does in relation to the presidency of the United States today. It contained offices for officials, meeting rooms, courts, and even cells where people charged with civil crimes could be held until their hearings.[30] In this initial hearing, Matthew reports that false charges were brought against Jesus and that witnesses came forward to testify against him. Jesus did not defend himself, but remained silent (see Matt. 26:63).[31]

73. *Cells in the Basement of a Church. These cells, used for noncapital offenders, are found in the lower level of St. Peter's in Gallicantu.*

What went on at this first hearing, the night Jesus was arrested? Rivkin offers some help here. He writes about the trial and execution of James, the brother of Jesus, but the same principle applies to the trial of Jesus, who was tried by the same council:

It is evident that, whatever the religious commitments of the members of this council may have been, when they served on the high priest's council, they served as political, not religious advisers.

Indeed, when Josephus uses the term sanhedrin in his writings, it always refers to a council appointed by an emperor, a king, or a high priest. He never uses the term when he is speaking of a permanent legislative body such as the Roman Senate. Such a body, he usually calls a boulé. Thus whenever Herod wished to have one of his sons, wives, or other relatives put to death for treason, he would convoke a sanhedrin, not a boulé. Such a sanhedrin based its judgment on political, not religious grounds.

Although Josephus does not specifically mention that Caiaphas convoked a sanhedrin, this does not mean that Caiaphas did not have a privy council; for Josephus says nothing about Caiaphas' priesthood, other than that he was the high priest. We may therefore assume that if Caiaphas had had to deal with a charismatic such as Jesus, he would have been unwilling to render a judgment without taking counsel with a sanhedrin, his privy council, which had only a political, not a religious function.[32]

Jesus was jailed overnight in the house of the high priest following the hearing. The following morning he was taken to the Temple Mount for a trial before the standing Sanhedrin, who would send him on to Pilate. Perhaps there were two charges against Jesus. Caiaphas and his privy council met to condemn him for sedition the night before. The larger group met to condemn him for blasphemy, thereby creating a situation in which the crowd could be swayed against Jesus.

What was the trial before the Jewish leaders like? We have no way of knowing for certain. Boers suggests that we look to the Mishnah for possible insights:

> We do not have written records from Jesus' time indicating the procedures to be followed in a Sanhedrin trial, but the subsequent recording of the oral traditions in the **Mishnah** provides valuable information. The gathering and editing of these rules were done by Jehuda the Patriarch, referred to in Jewish writings simply as Rabbi, who worked in Sepphoris [Zippori] in Galilee and lived from A.D. 135–220. Since the rules were written down

later we cannot be sure of the applicability of each one of them in the time of Jesus, but generally speaking we may assume that the rules recorded by Jehuda did apply at that time. Confirmation is provided in a number of cases by comparing the Lukan version of the trial of Jesus with those of Mark and Matthew.

One solution of the procedural inconsistencies is frequently offered but should be rejected at the outset: that the Sanhedrin was so intent on condemning Jesus that they disregarded their own rules. The Jewish leadership was evidently out to get Jesus, but we may take it as certain that they would have done so on the basis of their own legal codes, not in violation of them. Luke's alternate presentation of certain details in agreement with the rules described in the Mishnah suggests strongly that we look for another solution.

Especially in capital cases the Sanhedrin was intent on providing the best possible chance of acquittal. The following points from the tractate *Sanhedrin* 4:1, 5 and 5:2 are worth noting:

1. Noncapital cases were decided by three judges, capital cases by twenty-three.
2. In noncapital cases arguments could begin with reasons for either acquittal or conviction, but capital cases had to begin with reasons for acquittal.
3. In noncapital cases a verdict of either acquittal or conviction could be reached by a majority of one, but in capital cases only a verdict of acquittal could be reached by a majority of one. A verdict of conviction had to be reached by a majority of two.
4. In noncapital cases a verdict could be reversed from conviction to acquittal or from acquittal to conviction, but in capital cases a reversal could be made only from conviction to acquittal, not from acquittal to conviction.
5. In noncapital cases everyone could argue in favor of either acquittal or conviction, but in capital cases all could argue for acquittal but not in favor of conviction.
6. In noncapital cases a judge who had argued in favor of conviction could change his mind and argue in favor of acquittal, and vice versa, but in a capital case a change of argument could take place only in favor of acquittal.
7. In noncapital cases the trail was held in daytime and the verdict could be reached at night, but in capital cases the

trial had to be held in the daytime and the verdict also reached in the daytime.

8. In noncapital cases either verdict could be reached on the same day, but in capital cases only a verdict of acquittal could be reached on the same day. A verdict of conviction could not be reached until the next day.

9. In noncapital cases a witness could atone for a wrongful conviction by payment of money, but in capital cases a witness was answerable for the blood of a person wrongfully convicted.

10. In all cases, if witnesses contradicted each other their evidence became invalid.

To these we may add the following:

11. The punishment for blasphemy was stoning (*Sanh.* 7:4).

12. The rules for a conviction for blasphemy were very stringent. A person could not be found guilty unless he or she had actually pronounced the divine name itself. During the trial a substitute for the name of God was used in giving witness, but sentence could not be pronounced on the basis of the substitute name. All visitors were asked to leave the place of assembly, and the chief witness was then asked to say the precise words that had been pronounced by the accused, using the divine name itself. The other witnesses were then asked to confirm whether this was what the accused had said. The verdict was then reached on the basis of that witness. (*Sanh.* 7:5)

13. Even when a person was taken away to be stoned everything had to be done to ensure the possibility of a stay of execution if last-minute evidence in favor of the accused turned up. One person stood with a towel at the door of the court, and another, mounted on a horse, waited as far on the way to the place of execution as possible, but so that he could still see the person at the door. If someone in the court said that he or she still had something to argue in favor of acquittal, the man at the door had to wave the towel and the man on the horse then rushed to stay the execution. Even if the convicted person claimed to have something to add to the evidence, she or he had to be brought back and the trial had to resume. This procedure could occur up to five times. Even as the condemned was led forth to be stoned, a herald had to cry out, announcing

what the offense had been, who the witnesses were, and to request that if someone knew anything that would favor acquittal, such a one should come forward and plead the case of the convicted person (*Sanh.* 6:1).[33]

From all of this, Boers concludes that Luke's version of Jesus' trial before the Sanhedrin is more consistent with the requirements of the tractate *Mishnah Sanhedrin*. Furthermore, Boers points out that in Luke's account there is no conviction, no mistreatment of Jesus at the trial and that Jesus' trial is held during the day time (the morning after his arrest). In Luke's version, Jesus is sent to Pilate after a few preliminary questions.

Trial Before Pilate

Today there are three major theories as to the possible location of the trial of Jesus before Pilate. First, the traditional site of the trial is the courtyard of the Antonia Fortress, found today in the basement of the Sisters of Zion Convent in the Old City of Jerusalem. This traditional identification has, for the most part, been abandoned. Second, if Jesus was sent by Pilate to Herod

74. Herod's Palace. It is possible that Jesus was questioned by Pilate here.

Antipas, as Luke states, then the trial might have occurred at the Hasmonean Palace, located to the east of Herod the Great's palace, about halfway between the eastern wall of the city and Herod's palace. More than likely, Pilate made Herod's palace his residence when he would visit Jerusalem on special occasions. This would mean that Antipas would have had to find alternative quarters, and since he ranked equal to Pilate, he would have a comparable palatial residence. The Hasmonean Palace was the only other possibility. Some scholars in Israel (such as Pixner and B. Mazar) consider this site a viable option in this debate, but they are few in number. The third and most highly considered of the three choices today for the location of the trial of Jesus before Pilate would be the palace of Herod the Great, which Pilate made his residence in Jerusalem.

The Gospel writers go to great lengths to depict Pilate as being rather innocent in his dealings with Jesus, that he really wanted to release Jesus because he was so obviously innocent. However, history does not support the idea that Pilate was simply an innocent pawn in a grand, predestined drama. During his tenure as procurator, Pilate demonstrated over and over again his ruthlessness and his willingness to have people executed for little or no reason. Furthermore, on many occasions he found himself at odds with

75. Hasmonaean Palace. Jesus may have been questioned by Herod Antipas here.

the Jewish leadership. Josephus reports that one of these conflicts occurred when Pilate marched into Jerusalem with his troops carrying standards bearing the image of Emperor Tiberias. Jewish leaders were insulted by this act, for they considered it idolatry.[34] Later Pilate took money from the Temple treasury to fund a construction project to bring water into Jerusalem.[35] Menahem Stern reports that had it not been for Pilate's ruthlessness and cruelty he would not have been removed as procurator by Vitellius, the governor of Syria, in 36 CE.[36] The Gospel of Luke confirms Pilate's reputation for viciousness: "At that very time there were some present who told him about the Galileans whose blood Pilate had mingled with their sacrifices" (Luke 13:1). Make no mistake, Pilate would not hesitate to execute one Jewish peasant who was inciting the public.

Matthew, Mark, and John all report that Jesus was scourged before being sent out for execution. According to Jewish Law a person could receive up to forty lashes for various offenses.[37] In the basement/courtyard of the Sisters of Zion Convent, as well as in surrounding chapels, pieces of the game board of the "King's Game" have been preserved. Jesus was probably the victim of this cruel game, which was popular among soldiers stationed in Palestine in the first century. In this game a condemned

76. *"King's Game" Pavement. This game was played by Roman soldiers, using a mock king, a man condemned to death. The mock king would have been moved around a game board etched into a stone surface. This stone preserves the remains of such a game board and is found in the lower levels of the Sisters of Zion Convent in the Old City.*

77. The Church of the Holy Sepulchre

prisoner would be used as the game piece, being moved around a game board etched into the stone pavement. The movements were determined by a roll of the dice.

The "King's Game" apparently helped to boost the morale of soldiers posted in Judea, which was considered the worst assignment in the Roman army. By throwing dice, the soldiers would choose a burlesque "king"; following additional throws of the

150

dice, the "king" would be mocked and abused verbally and physically. The resemblance between this game and the mockery of Jesus by the soldiers reported in the Gospel (Matthew 27:27-31; Mark 15:16-20) is striking.[38]

The Execution of Jesus

Following his scourging, Jesus was handed over to the soldiers and led out to the place of execution. The traditional location of the execution of Jesus is found today beneath the Church of the Holy Sepulchre in the Old City of Jerusalem. There is so much evidence to support this site as the place of Jesus' crucifixion that little doubt can be cast on the matter. Let us consider a few reasons for making such a conclusion.

First of all, the execution site would have been located on a major thoroughfare or highway leading into and out of the city. This site was situated on the main road connecting Jerusalem and Caesarea. It was important to execute criminals and rebels in a place where the maximum public relations impact would be realized, and this was the most traveled highway into Jerusalem.

78. *Drawing of a First-century Boat. This is a drawing by an early pilgrim who visited the quarry beneath the Church of the Holy Sepulchre. This indicates that the tradition locating Jesus' burial and resurrection here is ancient.*

151

Second, we know that the place of execution was in a rock quarry located outside the city walls.[39] It was quite common to find the tombs of wealthy people in rock quarries such as this one; there are many such tombs in the Jerusalem area.[40] Even today one can find remains of first-century tombs inside the Church of the Holy Sepulchre, just to the west of the chapel commemorating the tomb of Jesus.

Third, archaeological evidence discovered in excavations in the early 1980s suggests that disciples came to this site to visit the tomb of their deceased teacher. Furthermore, behind the Chapel of St. Helena, in the lower level of the church, can be found the remains of what was likely a Judeo-Christian *miqvah*, or perhaps a baptismal pool, dating to the first century CE that may have been used by the followers of Jesus before they celebrated the Eucharist at the tomb site. Pottery pieces dating to the first century were found during the excavation work here; some of these shards are from bowls of the type that may have been used in the Last Supper. Other findings from this site include (1) an exterior wall from the Byzantine Church built by Queen Helena; (2) a large drain pipe that led from the Byzantine Church; (3) the wall of a very early room, which may have been used as a chapel or a house church; (4) a drawing on this same wall of a small first-century Roman fishing boat. Beneath the drawing is an inscription in Latin, which translates: "O Lord, we arrived."[41] This drawing indicates that followers of Jesus were coming to this site at a very early date. Finally, there is (5) the huge valley of the rock quarry, which surrounded the hill of Calvary.[42]

Finally, we have historical and traditional evidence to substantiate the claim that the execution and attested resurrection of Jesus occurred here. A brief and general review of the historical and traditional data might be helpful here. As stated above, this area was a large rock quarry. When quarrying was done here in the first century, the engineers discovered that some of the limestone was weak and not good for construction. As their quarrying progressed, a hill where this weak limestone was localized was left and a large valley emerged to surround this hill. The quarry completely surrounded this hill of weak, inadequate limestone. Eventually, as sections of the quarry yielded an inferior quality of stone, portions of the quarry were sold to be developed into tomb complexes for wealthy families. One of these tombs belonged to a follower of Jesus named Joseph of Arimathea (John 19:38), who offered his tomb as a burial place for Jesus. After the resurrection, followers of Jesus continued to come to this site to remember the death, burial, and resurrection of their leader and friend.

For the next one hundred years or so, even after the site had been brought into the city by Herod Agrippa, it remained

79. The Chapel of the Church of the Holy Sepulchre. The tomb of Jesus is memorialized in this chapel inside the Church of the Holy Sepulchre.

153

uncovered by any building. In approximately 135 CE, the Roman Emperor Hadrian had the quarry filled in and built on the site a temple and shrine honoring the goddess Aphrodite. Because of his hatred for the Christians and his hope that he could destroy their religious cult, Hadrian's goal was to eradicate any memory of Jesus' execution and burial site. Fortunately for us, however by building a temple on the site of Jesus' execution and burial, he preserved the memory of these events taking place on this site.

In the early fourth century, Queen Helena, mother of Constantine, embarked on a pilgrimage to the holy sites in Israel. When she arrived in Jerusalem she asked to see the place where Jesus had been executed, buried, and raised to life. She was taken to the temple built by Hadrian. Everyone knew exactly where to look because Hadrian had marked the location. Helena was so moved by the experience of visiting this holy place that she ordered a church to be built here. She was shown a slab of limestone that had been hewn out of the bedrock and was told that this was all that remained of Jesus' tomb. This slab became the central focus of the entire church. Construction on a chapel of the Holy Sepulchre began in 326 and the church built around it was dedicated in 335. Today, a similar stone preserves the memory of that fourth-century limestone.

Crucifixion was a commonly practiced form of execution in the first century. It was carried out on a permanent vertical beam to which would be attached a horizontal cross beam. This horizontal, or transverse, beam was bound with a strong rope to the victim, who was compelled to carry it to the place of execution. The horizontal beam, with victim attached, was then hoisted up and affixed to the vertical beam. The victim's feet were then nailed to the vertical beam. The bulk of the person's weight would rest against a small board or plank that was nailed to the side of the vertical beam. As a further degradation, victims were usually crucified in the nude. For Jews, this would have added humiliation to the physical pain of death. Usually this was a slow and extremely painful method of execution. Josephus writes of the capture and execution of a Jewish rebel named Eleazar, describing crucifixion as a horrible way to die.[43]

The Gospel accounts all agree that Jesus was executed by crucifixion and that both his hands and feet were nailed to the
cross beams, both horizontal and vertical beams. Jesus was
offered drugged vinegar or wine, perhaps to help relieve the
pain. According to the Gospel accounts, he died in the afternoon, just before the beginning of sabbath.

Burial and Mourning Practices

There is considerable information on death and mourning practices from rabbinic literature. One of the first acts by family and
friends at the discovery of the death of a loved one was to rend, or
tear, a small portion of their clothing. This custom survives today.
Families would gather, much like today, and preparations would
be made for the interment of the body. It was the common custom
of the day that bodies be buried before nightfall (see Acts 5:6ff.). In
Jesus' case, because it was late in the day and the Sabbath was
nearing, the body could not properly be prepared for burial. So
his body was taken to a tomb and his followers would return after
the Sabbath to properly prepare him for burial. Jesus was buried
in a tomb complex belonging to Joseph of Arimathea. The fact that
Joseph owned a tomb in a quarry leads us to conclude that he was
a man of wealth and prominence.

*80. This type of tomb was known as a kokhim. These types of burial chambers are
found within the Holy Sepulchre Church.*

Shemuel Safrai offers a detailed account of first-century custom and law with respect to the burial preparation and interment practices:

> Preparation of the corpse for burial consisted mainly in washing it and wrapping it in shrouds. The Mishnah states that the corpse is anointed and rinsed. The body was first anointed with oil to clean it and this was followed by a bath with water. . . .
>
> The Gospel of John notes that as part of the preparation for Jesus' burial, his body was "bound in linen cloths with spices, as was the burial custom of the Jews.". . . .
>
> . . . The preparation of the corpse for burial further included trimming the hair, the only exception being unmarried girls, who were buried with their hair loose, just as brides were brought to their wedding. The body was wrapped in shrouds, which are frequently mentioned in Jewish sources. These were garments specially prepared, or freshly laundered, for the purpose of wrapping the dead. The Hebrew word for these burial garments . . . connotes wrapping and binding more than dress, as is indicated also by tractate Semahot: "Men may wrap and bind men but not women, but women may wrap and bind both men and women." [44]

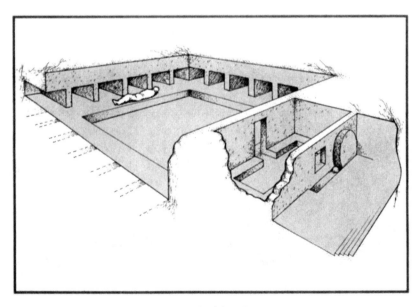

81. Tomb of the Kings

The most common way of interment practiced for the poor was simply to bury the body in the ground. Wealthy people's bodies were buried in tombs, hewn in the limestone quarries. These tombs were multichambered complexes containing many burial niches.[45] Immediately upon entering into a tomb complex, one would step into a large room used as a mourning chamber. Usually a bench would be hewn from the surrounding walls. Off of the mourning chamber would be other chambers. These secondary or auxiliary chambers would be used for the preparation of the bodies for interment. Surrounding the preparation chambers would be the actual rooms containing the burial niches, both *kokhim* or *arcosolia*.[46] Each niche would be sealed with a rectangular stone that fit exactly to the opening's dimensions. The entire complex would be sealed with a large, wheel-like stone, which would be rolled along a channel to secure the tomb complex.

Following the interment there were other customs to be observed, as Safrai relates:

> Following the burial a ceremony took place in which condolences were offered: the public ranged itself in a row, or rows, and the mourners passed among the rows while the public expressed their condolences. . . .
>
> Mourning practices were numerous and complex, some lasting thirty days, others for an entire year. The first seven days of mourning were the most serious: men and women sat shoeless on the ground or on low supports, and they were forbidden to work, wash, anoint themselves or engage in sexual intercourse; even the study of Torah was prohibited. Beds remained in their lowered positions during the entire week of mourning. . . . During the first three days of mourning, even the poor were forbidden to work. Some texts claim that during the first three days a mourner was also forbidden to put on phylacteries [*tefillin*], for the impact of his bereavement came during those days.[47]

Other Aspects of the Judean Ministry

Several reported events in the ministry of Jesus that are set in Judea do not fit into the chronological sequence suggested

82. Photograph of a Rolling Stone. Tomb complexes containing kokhim were sealed with a rolling stone such as this one.

above. Since our understanding of these stories is enhanced through the analysis of first-century Jewish peasant culture, these stories or passages will be reviewed here.

Luke appears to be geographically confused in his presentation of the events contained in Luke 10 and 11, or at least there is a sudden shift from Galilee to Judea. Luke 10 (and before) is set in the north. Suddenly, in Luke 10:38ff., we are told that Jesus was in Judea. There is no transition.[48] Jesus unexpectedly appeared in Bethany, where he had a discussion with Mary and Martha concerning priorities.

Following his meeting with Mary and Martha, we are told, "he was praying at a certain place, and when he had ceased, one of his disciples said to him, 'Lord, teach us to pray, as John taught his disciples' " (Luke 11:1). Jesus responded by teaching the disciples the Lord's Prayer. This event is remembered today at the Church of Pater Noster (or the Eleona Church) on the Mount of Olives, located between Bethany and Jerusalem:

> Within the courtyard of the Church of Pater Noster is a cave. According to an early Christian tradition, now generally discounted, Jesus taught his disciples secretly in this cave. The apocryphal Acts of John claim that Jesus did teach his disciples in a cave locate somewhere on the Mount of Olives; this could be the source of the early Christian tradition. Both the Bordeaux Pilgrim (333 CE) and Egeria (381–384 CE) report in their journals that they visited this cave.
>
> Queen Helena, mother of Constantine, ordered the building of the Church of Eleona in the mid-fourth century CE. The name Eleona is a corruption of the Greek word *elaion*, which means "olives." This church was destroyed during the Persian invasion of 614 CE. In 1102, after Jerusalem had been taken by the Crusaders, two marble slabs were found, upon which were written the Lord's Prayer in Hebrew and Greek. It was assumed that this must have been the place where Jesus taught his disciples the Lord's Prayer.[49]

83. Church of Pater Noster. This church is the traditional cite of Jesus' teaching the Lord's Prayer to his disciples. It is located on the Mt. of Olives.

From Jesus' frequent use of the Eremos Cave between Capernaum and Gennesaret, we may conclude that Jesus had a fondness for caves, or at least quiet places away from the crowds. Caves like these would give him privacy. (The Cave of Gethsemane [Cave of the Betrayal] is located at the foot of the Mount of Olives.) It is not unthinkable that Jesus might have been in this cave, from time to time, with his disciples. However, we would have to expect that Jesus taught the Lord's Prayer to the disciples in Galilee.

Luke 11 also places other very familiar teaching lessons of Jesus in this setting; some of them parallel aspects of the Sermon on the Mount (Luke 11:9-13, 33-36). Also set here is the discussion concerning the request for a sign: "This generation is an evil generation; it asks for a sign, but no sign will be given to it except the sign of Jonah. For just as Jonah became a sign to the people of Nineveh, so the Son of Man will be to this generation" (Luke 11:29-30). Jesus' reply has been misrepresented by some scholars and preachers in the West. Some understand the sign of Jonah, being in the belly of a fish for three days, as relating to Jesus' being entombed for three days. The Middle Eastern interpretation of this passage is that the sign of Jonah means that the word of God will be going out to foreigners. Later in Luke 11 we have the report of the confrontation and condemnation by Jesus of the scribes and Pharisees reported in Matthew 23 (discussed above).

A second story related to the Judean ministry is that of Jesus' healing of a paralyzed man at the Pools of Bethesda, reported in John 5:2-9. According to the story, Jesus was passing by the Bethesda Pools when he encountered a man who had been paralyzed for thirty-eight years. The man complained that he had no one to put him into the water after it had been stirred.[50] It is important to remember that it is a violation of the Jewish Law of ritual purity for a person to visit a pagan place, and the man's presence here would have been considered idolatry, because the Bethesda Pools were located within a Roman temple dedicated to the god Serapis, the god of healing.[51] This temple was located just to the east of the Antonia Fortress, and so it probably functioned much like a contemporary military chapel for the soldiers stationed in Jerusalem. One of the daily rituals at a Serapis temple was as follows: In the early morning a priest

84. The Pools of Bethesda. This is the site of Jesus' healing of a paralyzed man. John's Gospel mentions five porticoes here, which were a part of a pagan Roman temple dedicated to the god Serapis. The temple probably functioned much like a military chapel for troops.

of the cult would throw a snake into the pool of water located at the temple. (Throughout antiquity the snake was believed to have curative powers.) A tradition of the cult held that the first person to get into the water after the snake had been thrown in would be healed. The paralyzed man whom Jesus met complained that he had no one to help him into the water, alluding to this custom. Jesus pronounced the man healed and told him to take his pallet and go home.

A third event worth mentioning is the healing of a blind man. Jesus made a mud pack from clay and spittle, rubbed it onto the man's eyes, and told him to go and wash his eyes in the Pool of Siloam. (The Pool of Siloam was located south of the Temple Mount, near the gate adjacent to the Kidron and Hinnom Valleys.) This pool was the repository for the waters of the Gihon Springs and was fed by the water channel constructed by King Hezekiah in the seventh century BCE. Finally, let us discuss the teaching related to John 10, the teaching pertaining to shepherding and the function of the sheepfold. In the first century, shepherding was considered a despised trade, and those who were employed as shepherds were automatically branded as unclean. Joachim Jeremias, in his landmark work *Jerusalem in the Time of Jesus*, writes:

161

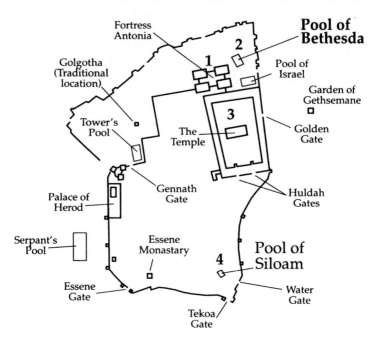

85. Map of the Pools of Bethesda, Including Siloam. 1. The Antonia Fortress 2. The Pools of Betheseda 3. The Temple Mount 4. The Pool of Siloam

Although the question of racial purity determined to a large extent the social position of the Jew of New Testament times within his own community, we must not conclude ... that this question was the only determining factor. As we have already seen ... an inferior position because of blood or social rank was by no means prejudicial to the social position of the scribes. Conversely, we must show in the following pages that there were circumstances—quite independent of ancestry—which carried a social stigma in public opinion. First of all, there was a whole series of trades which were despised, and those who practised them were, to a greater or less degree, exposed to social degradation.[52]

Why would shepherding be considered such a lowly trade? Several centuries earlier it had been thought of as a noble occupation. Jeremias suggests that shepherds were, for the most part, thought of as thieves and generally dishonest. If an animal were lost, they might not go and look for it. They might steal an animal and report that it was lost or taken by a lion. He points out that the Oral Law forbade the purchase of milk and wool from a shepherd. In spite of their lowly status, Jesus uses them as an example of God's loving care, and his own.

The sheepfold, an image Jesus used prominently, functioned in a very specific way in the first century (and it continues to function in much the same manner today). Across the opening of a cave, or natural cleft that was not very deep, shepherds would create a wall from loose stones. The wall would be a little over a meter in height. Along the top of the wall, shepherds would place thick branches with thorns, which would serve as a deterrent for predatory animals who might try to steal the animals. In this wall the shepherd would leave a small opening that would function as an entrance into and out of the sheepfold. The shepherd would stand in this opening and call the sheep, one by one, to come. The sheep would be inspected for thorns or briars in its wool, which would be promptly removed, and for cuts, bruises, or sores on their bodies, which would be cleaned and salved. Once the last sheep had been properly checked and brought safely into the sheepfold, the shepherd would sit or squat in the opening, literally becoming the gate or door to the sheepfold. Jesus suggests that this is how he will care for the people in God's sheepfold.

86. A Sheepfold Near Bethlehem

EPILOGUE:
THE RESURRECTION OF JESUS

The resurrection of Jesus is the single defining theological belief in the Christian church. Individual Christians in numerous denominations may disagree over many theological concepts, but one common thread links together all Christian communities: belief in the resurrection of Jesus.

All of the Gospels report that Jesus was miraculously raised from death on the Sunday following his execution on the previous Friday (see Matthew 28; Mark 16; Luke 24; and John 20–21). The Gospel accounts disagree on the details and report different witnesses to the event, but agree that the risen Jesus appeared to all of the disciples and many of his closer friends and family.

The Place of the Burial and Resurrection

There has been considerable debate over the last century or so concerning the site of the burial and resurrection of Jesus. The two most popular possible locations are Gordon's Calvary and the Church of the Holy Sepulchre.

Gordon's Calvary

The Garden Tomb, the only Protestant shrine in the Holy Land, was discovered by General Charles Gordon in 1883. He believed that the rugged hill to the north of the present-day city walls of the Old City resembled a skull, and he announced that he had found Golgotha. Adjacent to the "skull hill" is a small tomb complex, which Gordon identified as the tomb of Jesus. Unfortunately, this identification is based more on Christian piety and Protestant hopes of having a holy shrine in the Land than on tradition or fact. At best, this is a quiet place where Christian pilgrims may come to pray away from the noise and busy activity of Jerusalem.

Scholars disagree on the dating of the tomb found here. Some have suggested that the tomb dates to the Iron Age, roughly to the eighth or ninth centuries BCE Others date the tomb to the Byzantine Period, in roughly the fourth century CE It has also been argued that the tomb is an Iron Age tomb that was reconstructed in the Byzantine Period. About the only thing we can say with some certainty is that the tomb in no way resembles the typical burial tombs common to Judea from the first century BCE through the middle part of the second century CE, and could not have been used during the time of Jesus.

Church of the Holy Sepulchre

The Church of the Holy Sepulchre is the holiest shrine of Christendom. The church is built over the most likely site of the execution, burial, and resurrection of Jesus. This identification is supported by history, tradition, and archaeology.

First, as was noted above, the site was used as a stone quarry until the early first century CE, and it was common for wealthy people to use abandoned quarries like this one for tomb complexes. There are many examples of tomb complexes for the wealthy and prominent in quarries in and around Jerusalem (the Tomb of the Kings or the Tomb of Queen Helena of Adiabene, the Sanhedrin Tombs, Herod's Family Tomb, etc.). The Gospels report that Jesus was buried in a tomb that belonged to Joseph of Arimathea, a wealthy and prominent member of the Jewish Council known as the Sanhedrin. Even today the remains of such tombs can be found within the Church of the Holy Sepulchre.

Second, its location just outside the city walls of first-century CE Jerusalem fits the description of the site of Jesus' crucifixion and burial as "place of the skull" with nearby graves (John 19:17).

Third, early Christian traditions identifying this site as the actual place of Jesus' burial led Constantine's mother, Queen Helena, to select it for the first Church of the Holy Sepulchre, which was completed and dedicated in 335 CE. The Byzantine structure was destroyed in 1009 CE by Muslim forces during their occupation of Jerusalem, and the present church is based on the one rebuilt by the Crusaders in 1149 CE. Six Christian groups (Roman Catholics, Greek Orthodox, Armenians, Syrians, Copts, and Ethiopians) now share control of the present church, which contains twenty-two different chapels.

For almost 2,000 years, then, Christians have reverenced this site. The present tomb monument dates from the nineteenth century, but a fragment of the original fourth-century monument can be seen in the base of the Coptic shrine. The remains of a Jewish tomb from the first century, with burial shafts (cut into the seams of the old quarry workings) and ossuary pits, can be seen from the Syrian chapel.

Jesus' Postresurrection Appearances

The accounts of Jesus' postresurrection appearances in the Gospels of Matthew and Mark are brief. Matthew's account (28:1-20) tells of an angel rolling the stone away from the mouth of the tomb, then of Jesus appearing to Mary Magdalene and the "other Mary" and instructing them to tell the disciples to go to Galilee, where they later see Jesus on a mountain, and where he gives them the "great commission" and promises to be with them forever. Mark's account ends with Mary, Mary Magdalene, and Salome running away from the empty tomb in fear (16:8; the material in Mark 16:9-20 is thought by many scholars to have been added to the original Gospel account at a later date). The more extensive accounts are in the Gospels of Luke and John.

The Gospel of Luke

Luke tells the story of the encounter between the risen Jesus and two followers, one who is named Cleopas. Cleopas and an unnamed companion were walking from Jerusalem to their home village of Emmaus on the first Easter Sunday. Jesus appeared to them but was not recognized. They walked along together discussing the events of the past days, Cleopas summarizing them for the unidentified stranger who seemed to be unaware of all that had happened. When they finally arrived in Emmaus, Cleopas invited their traveling companion to stay with them for dinner and the evening. Jesus blessed and broke the bread for the meal, was instantly recognized, and then suddenly vanished from their sight. The two men from Emmaus then returned to Jerusalem where they told the disciples and friends of Jesus just what they had experienced.

There are at least three possible locations for biblical Emmaus, and, in truth, no one can identify the location with any certainty. The sites with the strongest traditions are Latrun, Abu Ghosh, and Qubeiba.

The ruins of a Byzantine and Crusader monastery and basilica that were built over a site traditionally identified with Emmaus date to the fourth century CE. Today this place is known as Latrun, and it is located some eighteen miles (30 km.) west of Jerusalem, just off of the main highway connecting Jerusalem and Tel Aviv.

Prior to the Six Day War, in 1967, an Arab village known as Imwas was located on this site. The name Imwas remembered or preserved the name of the biblical village Emmaus. In the early third century CE, the name of the village was changed to Nicopolis. Early Church leaders such as Eusebius and Jerome wrote about Jesus' encounter with Cleopas and his companion in this place, and at this time Nicopolis became a place of pilgrimage for Christians.

During the Byzantine Period (in the early 4th century CE), a church and monastery were established here. The ruins of a Byzantine church with its beautiful mosaics are still preserved. The Crusaders also built a church on the site of the Byzantine church. The ruins of this church are also found adjacent to the Byzantine ruins.

During the first century CE, and before, a healthy adult could travel a minimum of twenty miles a day by walking. Latrun, as stated above, is located some eighteen miles (30 km.) west of

Jerusalem and is within this range. However, this site and distance is problematic. We must assume that Cleopas and his friend began their journey late in the morning, perhaps even in the afternoon. This would make it difficult to travel the distance from Jerusalem to Latrun (Emmaus-Nicopolis), and arrive in the early evening. Therefore, locating biblical Emmaus here at Latrun is questionable.

A second possible location for biblical Emmaus is Qubeiba. This tradition dates to the Crusades, with no evidence of any Byzantine identification of the site as Emmaus.

A third possibility is in locating Emmaus near present-day Abu Ghosh. This was the location of the Old Testament village of Kirjath-jearim (1 Sam. 7:2), where the Ark of the Covenant was kept after being returned by the Philistines. As with Qubeiba, the Crusaders identified this place as a possible location for Emmaus. A Crusader church was also built here commemorating Jesus' encounter with Cleopas and his companion. Abu Ghosh is located some seven miles (roughly 12 km.) east of Jerusalem, just off the main highway to Tel Aviv. This distance makes this a more attractive possibility than Latrun. However, there is no evidence that this tradition dates before the Crusades.

In the final analysis, we really have no idea where the biblical Emmaus was located. The earliest tradition is Latrun, which continues to be the most popular pilgrim site for modern visitors to Israel.

The Gospel of John

The resurrection account in the Gospel of John reports that on the first Easter Sunday, Mary Magdalene came to the tomb of Jesus and found the body missing. She came to Peter and told him that the body of Jesus had been taken away. Peter and an unidentified disciple (perhaps John), who had been hiding with the other disciples and followers of Jesus, came to the tomb and found it empty. After Peter and the unidentified disciple left the tomb and returned to their hiding place, two angels appeared to Mary and finally the risen Jesus also appeared, revealing himself to her. Mary then returned to the disciples and told them of her experience.

In the evening of that same day, Jesus appeared to most of the disciples in the room where they were hiding. John goes on to report the well-known story of "doubting Thomas," who was not present with the others at the first appearance of Jesus, and who frankly refused to believe their account of Jesus' appearance to them until Jesus appeared also to him.

In John 21 the disciples returned to Galilee. Their leader had been executed, and it appeared that the new work was now over. There was nothing for them to do except to return to the families and their occupations. In saying to his colleagues, "I am going fishing," Peter is saying, "It is time to return to the normal routine of my daily life as a husband, father, fisherman, and brother." The other disciples agree with him, and they too return to their pre-Jesus lifestyles (see John 21:3).

The following morning the disciples returned to their fishing in the coves south of Capernaum, perhaps in one of the coves where the disciples were first called to follow Jesus (Mark 1:16ff.). As they were fishing, Jesus appeared on the shore, but the disciples did not recognze him. Jesus asked if they had caught anything, and they said that they had not. He directed them to throw their nets out into the water on the other side of their boats, where they realized a large catch.

There was nothing particularly miraculous about this advice from Jesus. Standing on the shore of the Sea of Galilee from the area of the Primacy Church near Tabgha, one can easily see fish schooling near the surface of the water that would not be visible to people who would be fishing in a boat. Many Israeli fishermen today rely on people on the bank to point out such schools of fish from the bank.

Following this big catch, the "disciple whom Jesus loved" told Peter that the stranger on the shore who had pointed out the school of fish was, in fact, Jesus. Peter swam to the shore, and the other disciples came in their boats. On the shore, Jesus and the disciples shared a meal. Jesus then taught the disciples and challenged Peter to "feed my sheep." The book comes to a close with Jesus and the disciples in Galilee on the shore of the Sea of Galilee.

The Ascension of Jesus

None of the Gospels have much to say about the ascension. Matthew ends with Jesus' mountaintop promise to be with the disciples "to the end of the age" (Matt 28:20). Unless one accepts the material in the so-called longer ending of Mark (16:9-20) as authentic, Mark also does not report the ascension of Jesus; even the longer ending simply says that Jesus was "taken up into heaven" (Mark 16:19) and does not specify where this happened. Luke tells of Jesus leading the disciples from Jerusalem "out as far as Bethany" and giving them his final blessing, following which "he withdrew from them and was carried up into heaven" (Luke 24:50-51). John closes with the risen Jesus and his disciples together beside the Sea of Galilee.

In Acts 1:4, however, we are informed that the disciples remained in Jerusalem, following instructions from the risen Jesus. In Acts 1:12 we find that the ascension of Jesus is set here, on the Mount of Olives. This tradition is preserved today in a place known as the Mosque of the Ascension.

NOTES

1. The Land and Jesus

1. Yohanan Aharoni, *The Land of the Bible: A Historical Geography* (Philadelphia: Westminster Press, 1979), 220.

2. James R. Beasley, et al., *An Introduction to the Bible* (Nashville: Abingdon Press, 1991), 124-25.

3. Some do not consider Saul a true king. He certainly did not function as a king in any real sense. Under Saul there was no centralized standing army, no capital, no taxation. He lived in a rustic fortress in Gibeah, just to the north of Jerusalem, and functioned more as a warlord than a king.

4. There is some debate concerning whether Alexander had a hand in his father's death. See William G. Sinnigen and Charles Alexander Robinson, *Ancient History* (New York: Macmillan, 1981), 257: "By divorcing Olympias (Alexander's mother) and marrying the noblewoman Cleopatra in 337 BC. Alexander's former admiration of his father turned to repugnance. Philip and his son were estranged because although a Macedonian prince normally expected his father to have casual amours, formal marriage to another woman might potentially threaten his own succession. Both Alexander and his mother were forced to leave Pella, she for her native Epirus, he for Illyrai, although he was permitted to return after a superficial reconciliation was arranged with Philip. Alexander's position was nevertheless insecure." Sinnigen goes on to report that rumors circulated at that time that Alexander engineered his father's death.

5. Charles R. Page II and Carl A. Volz, *The Land and the Book: An Introduction to the World of the Bible* (Nashville: Abingdon Press, 1993), 52.

6. There is a very detailed account of the events leading up to and through the Maccabbean Revolt in the books of Maccabees and in the writings of Josephus.

7. See Daniel 9:27; 11:31-45; 1 Maccabees 1:36-40.

8. The Jewish celebration of Hanukkah comes from this rededication of the Temple. There are at least two stories of the meaning of Hanukkah. Rabbi Hayim Donin writes, "Hanukkah is observed for eight days, beginning with the twenty-fifth day of Kislev. It commemorates the historic victory of the Maccabeans following the three-year long uprising against the ruling Assyrian-Greek regime and their Jewish Hellenist supporters who conspired to impose restrictions against Jewish religious practices and values. The struggle

culminated with the recapture of the Temple of Jerusalem in 165 BCE and the restoration of its traditional Jewish service. The victory also restored Jewish political sovereignty over the land. Hanukkah means dedication and refers to the rededication of the Temple to the service of God after it had been defiled with pagan images and practices" (Hayim Donin, *To Be a Jew: A Guide to Jewish Observance in Contemporary Life* [New York: Basic Books, 1972], 258).

Another tradition holds that when the Temple had been recaptured there was only enough oil to burn the candle over the ark of the covenant for one day. Miraculously, the candle remained lit for eight days until additional oil was made available. Following this miracle a holiday was declared, the Festival of Lights, to memorialize the miracle. This tradition is affirmed by more conservative Jewish people.

In Reform or Progressive traditions Hanukkah is celebrated as freedom from oppression. The real miracle, they claim, is that a small, poorly armed and poorly trained guerrilla army could defeat a well-trained, well-armed group of professional soldiers. The miracle has nothing to do with lights and oil, but rather with freedom for Jewish people.

9. The Maccabean Dynasty is also known as the Hasmonean Dynasty, after the family name.

10. Shemuel Safrai and Menahem Stern, eds., *The Jewish People in the First Century*, 2 vols. (Assen: Van Gorcum; Philadelphia: Fortress Press, 1974–76), 1:87-88.

11. The Edomites were driven from their territory, in what is today southern Jordan, by the Nabataeans in the fourth century BCE. They relocated their home in the Negev of southern Palestine. When this territory came under the control of the Hasmonaeans, the Idumaeans were forced to convert to Judaism and to submit to circumcision.

12. The Christians referred to Jewish followers of Jesus as Nazarenes. Jewish people called these same persons the *Minim*, usually translated "heretics." See Ray A. Pritz, *Nazarene Jewish Christianity* (Jerusalem: Magnes Press/Hebrew University Press, 1992), for an excellent general introduction into the Nazarene sect.

13. Babylonian Talmud, Sanhedrin 43.

14. *Desposyni* refers to a servant who belongs to a master and was used in the early church to refer to the relationship between believers and the risen Christ.

15. Eusebius Pamphilus, *Ecclesiastical History* (Grand Rapids: Baker Book House, 1987), 34.

16. Cochaba (or Kochba) was a small village found in first-century Batanea (Old Testament Bashan), on the eastern side of the Sea of Galilee not far from the ancient pilgrim route from Babylon to Judea. Its name means "the star" or "the star village." The name itself has strong messianic overtones. Perhaps this village was first settled by Davidic descendants after the edict of Cyrus in 539 BCE.

17. The Via Maris, or The Way of the Sea, was probably the most important trade route in the western Fertile Crescent. This trade route passed through ancient Palestine, literally making the Land a bridge that connected Africa, Asia, and Europe. Every passing caravan had to cross through this land. The trade route passed through some of biblical Palestine's most fertile farming land. Therefore, the land through which the trade route passed was some of

the most valuable and fought-for land in antiquity. Those who controlled this strategically important area monopolized commerce, trade, and farming. This was an important source of revenue for the dominant power.

18. Bargil Pixner, *With Jesus Through Galilee According to the Fifth Gospel* (Rosh Pina: Chorazin Press, 1992), 16-17.

19. The village of Nazareth is located on a hill overlooking the Jezreel Valley, one of the most fertile areas of the western Fertile Crescent. There are three primary classifications for ancient settlements:: village, town, and city. Communities with less than 2,500 people were classified as villages. Unfortified settlements with populations exceeding 2,500 were usually classified as towns. Fortified centers with larger populations were called cities. There were few cities in the country during the first century CE. Among them were Jerusalem, Caesarea Maritima, Zippori (Sepphoris), and Tiberias.

20. Richard A. Batey, *Jesus and the Forgotten City* (Grand Rapids: Baker Book House, 1991), 66-76, among others, offers an excellent general discussion on the nature of carpentry in the first century CE. He points out that the Greek word *tekton,* used in the Septuagint, has been erroneously translated as "carpenter" in the English translations of the Gospels. He suggests that a better translation of the word might be "artisan," which should be understood as a skilled worker or one who works with his hands in the construction industry. The *tekton* might work with one of several materials, such as wood, stone, or ivory. But in first century Palestine, most houses and other buildings were constructed of stone, just as in Israel today. Therefore, it may be more appropriate to think of Joseph as a stone mason rather than a carpenter per se. This is not to say that he might not have had a small workshop where he made furniture or tools.

21. Josephus suggests that some of the crops grown in these small family gardens were also used to pay taxes (see *Antiquities of the Jews* 14:202ff.).

22. In Israel it is commonly believed that John the Baptist ate carob and honey rather than locusts and honey. Even today carob is colloquially known as St. John's Bread, which is a staple among the poor.

2. Prelude to Ministry

1. See Herbert Danby, trans., *The Mishnah* (London: Oxford University Press, 1987), 227 (Mishnah Yebamoth 6:6).

2. David Flusser, *The Spiritual History of the Dead Sea Sect* (Tel Aviv: Mod Books, 1989), 31.

3. Danby, *The Mishnah,* 245.

4. Ibid., 224.

5. Hendrikus Boers, *Who Was Jesus? The Historical Jesus and the Synoptic Gospels* (New York: Harper & Row, 1989), 8.

6. Danby, *The Mishnah,* 116.

7. Ibid., 190.

8. There are Mishnaic requirements as well as the requirements of the Law for making specific offerings after childbirth. See Mishnah Kerithoth 1:3 ff. and Mishnah Kinnim 1:1. The Torah also has certain requirements, found in Leviticus 12:1-8.

9. Shemuel Safrai and Menahem Stern, eds., *The Jewish People in the First Century*, 2 vols. (Assen: Van Gorcum; Philadelphia: Fortress Press, 1974–76), 2:766-67.

10. Ibid., 769.

11. Babylonian Talmud, Shabbath 130.

12. For an excellent discussion of contemporary circumcision practices in Judaism and the naming of male children, see Hayim Donin, *To Be a Jew: A Guide to Jewish Observance in Contemporary Life* (New York: Basic Books, 1972), 271, 273-76.

13. An early Eastern church tradition holds that this announcement was made near a spring in Nazareth. Today the spring is found inside a beautiful Orthodox Church in the city.

14. The ruins of biblical Sepphoris (known in Hebrew as Zippori) are being excavated under the auspices of the Israeli Ministry of Antiquities. The site is one of the major excavations now taking place in Israel. Prominent American scholars working on the dig include James F. Strange, Carol Myers, and Eric Myers. Batey, *Jesus and the Forgotten City* (Grand Rapids: Baker Book House, 1991), provides an excellent introduction to Zippori and its importance.

15. The *Protevangelium Jacobi* is better known in English as the *Gospel of James*. We are told here that Mary was made a "ward" of Joseph in the following manner:

> And behold, an angel of the Lord appeared saying, "Zacharias, Zacharias, go out and call together the widowers of the people, and let each of them bring a rod; and whomever the Lord God shows a sign, to this one shall she [Mary] be wife." The heralds therefore went through the whole of the Jewish countryside and sounded the trumpet of the Lord, and all came running. Now Joseph . . . came himself into their meeting. When they were all gathered together, they came to the priest, taking their rods. He, having received the rods of all of them, went into the Temple and prayed. When he finished the prayer he took the rods and came out and returned them; and there was no sign on them. Joseph received the last rod, and behold, a dove came forth from the rod and settled on Joseph's head. Then the priest said, "Joseph, Joseph, you have been designated by lot to receive the virgin of the Lord as your ward." (*Protevangelium Jacobi* 8:7–9:4).

For an excellent translation of the *Protevangelium Jacobi*, see Cartlidge and Dungan, *Documents for the Study of the Gospels* (Philadelphia: Fortress Press, 1980), 107-17.

The *Protevangelium Jacobi* is considered by most scholars to be a second-century CE work. However, this writing demonstrates that at least as early as the second century CE there was a tradition that located Mary and her family's home in Judaea.

This story is probably the result of the early church's attempt to explain Jesus' brothers and sisters. Matthew 13:55-56 mentions Jesus' brothers' names and states that they are his "brothers." The early church, however, interpreted these relatives as cousins or stepbrothers from Joseph's earlier marriage(s), suggesting that Joseph and Mary never had sexual intercourse and that Mary had no other children. It is probable that the *Protevangelium Jacobi* is no more than theologized history.

16. The custom of a father's providing a home for his each son and his wife following their marriage is still practiced in the Middle East today. In fact,

there are many parallels between first-century and twentieth-century peasant culture, particularly among the Bedouin, the nomadic shepherds who inhabit the region. Kenneth Bailey writes: "In the south of Egypt, in the mountains of Lebanon, and in the isolated communities of upper Syria and Iraq, there are peasant communities which have lived in remarkable isolation from the rest of the world. It is not only their isolation which has enabled them to preserve ancient ways of life, however, but also they regard changelessness as being of highest value. This principle is of great antiquity and is not unknown in the Bible. . . . To preserve meaning was to preserve the status quo. This identity of value and changelessness has maintained itself in the Middle Eastern peasant society all through the centuries" (Kenneth E. Bailey, *Poet and Peasant and Through Peasant Eyes* [Grand Rapids: Eerdmans, 1983], 31). Bailey goes on to add, "Everybody knows how everybody is expected to act in any given situation" (35).

17. For a discussion of the types of homes found in first-century CE Nazareth, see Jean Briand, *The Judeo-Christian Church of Nazareth* (Jerusalem: Franciscan Press, 1982). This is also an excellent general introduction to the excavations beneath the Latin Church of the Annunciation.

18. Understanding how an insula functioned can help us to better understand the implications of several of Jesus' teachings. For example, in Luke 11:5-8 we read: "And he said to them, 'Suppose one of you has a friend, and you go to him at midnight and say to him, "Friend, lend me three loaves of bread; for a friend of mine has arrived, and I have nothing to set before him." And he answers from within, "Do not bother me; the door has already been locked, and my children are with me in bed; I cannot get up and give you anything." I tell you, even though he will not get up and give him anything because he is his friend, at least because of his persistence he will get up and give him whatever he needs.' "

Knowing that the families were large and that the members all slept together in one small room helps us to better understand this teaching. Literally the room would have been filled with sleeping children and it would have been physically impossible for anyone to negotiate the limited walking space in a dark room to assist a friend at midnight. Thus Jesus' point is that God does go through such trouble for us. Jesus goes on to say, "Ask, and it will be given you; search, and you will find; knock, and the door will be opened for you" (Luke 11:9).

Also, in Luke 15:8-10, we find the parable of the woman with a lost coin. The Gospel writer presupposes that readers will be familiar with the houses and living conditions of the people. However, understanding that they lived in insulae and that the majority of persons were very poor helps us to better place this parable in a historical/cultural context. It would have been very difficult, if not impossible, for anyone to find a small coin in a dark sleeping chamber in an insula with an irregular stone floor. Yet, again, if you seek you will find. Jesus' point is that God comes and looks for the lost with the same kind of dedication that it took for the woman to find a coin in just such a house.

19. Safrai and Stern, *The Jewish People in the First Century,* 2:771-72.

20. Danby, *The Mishnah,* 750-51.

21. The Wilderness of Judea is a geographical region found in Israel. The word *wilderness* is not an adjective meant to describe a barren place, although

the Wilderness of Judea is certainly barren and desolate. It covers the region from just north of Jericho and bordering on Jerusalem on the eastern side and stretches southward to the Negev Desert.

22. *Miqvot* have been found in the basement of the Church of the Annunciation in Nazareth, in Chorazim, under the Holy Sepulchre Church, near the teaching steps at the southern end of the Temple Mount, in the Herodion Fortress, at Masada, and in great abundance in the ruins at Qumran. The Essenes were passionate about ritual purity. This is why we find many *miqvot* in Qumran, along with the elaborate water system that supports them.

23. Josephus discusses the long process for becoming a member of the Essene sect in *The Jewish War* 2:137-54.

24. The ruins of Herod's winter palace are found today in Tulul Abu el-Alaiq, just to the south and west of modern-day Jericho. This was one of the largest of Herod's palace complexes, consisting of seven or eight large palace-like buildings, gardens, pools, and baths.

25. There were two dominant schools of thought within the Pharisee movement during the first century CE. These were the schools, or houses, of Hillel and Shammai. The House of Hillel was more left leaning, or liberal, in its theology and interpretation of the law (both oral and written). The House of Shammai was more conservative. Even then, however, the house of Shammai was much more moderate than the Hasidim.

26. It is possible that Jesus, Andrew, and the unnamed follower spent the night in Kochaba, a village in Batanea (or Bethany beyond the Jordan). Since there was a theological as well as a cultural tie between Nazareth and Kochaba, Jesus would have been among members of his clan and people with whom he had a common bond.

27. The Middle Bronze Period was approximately 2000–1550 BCE, the Late Bronze Period was roughly 1550–1200 BCE, the Persian Period corresponds roughly to the Late Iron III, 600–332 BCE, and the Hellenistic Period was 333–63 BCE. There is still considerable debate on the dating of the Hellenistic Period. Some scholars contend that the Hellenistic Period ends with the rise of the Hasmonean Dynasty. Others date the Hellenistic Period to the invasion of Pompey in 63 BCE. Still others do not believe that the Hellenistic Period should be dated along historical lines at all but as a cultural phenomenon and that we are still living under the influences of Hellenism today. The dates listed here close the Hellenistic Period with the invasion of Pompey in 63 BCE.

28. The earlier excavations were carried out by Kohl and Watzinger. They discovered the synagogue and worked there until the beginning of World War I. But the major excavation was done by Father Virgil Corbo and Loffreda between 1968 and 1985. See Charles R. Page II and Carl A. Volz, *The Land and the Book: An Introduction to the World of the Bible* (Nashville: Abingdon Press, 1993), 122-26.

29. These millstones were made of the basalt stone, common to the area. Basalt stones have also been found in excavations in the south in places such as the Herodion Fortress near Bethlehem. This industry must have been very successful.

30. This is confirmed by the presence of a tax office and a Roman centurion who was stationed there to ensure that the taxes were collected without any difficulty (see Matthew 17:24; Luke 7:1-10).

31. Four types of civil taxes were collected by the government: (1) an income tax (or a tax on crops, etc.; see Josephus *Antiquities* 17:205); (2) a poll tax (or registration or census tax; see Matthew 22:15-22; and Luke 2:1ff.); (3) a sales tax (see Josephus *Antiquities* 17:205); and the (4) frontier tax (money collected when anyone crossed international borders (see Matthew 17:25; Luke 19:1-10; Romans 13:7). Capernaum, located on the border with Gaulinitus, would have been the collection station for this tax on people traveling from the territories of Antipas and Philip. Jericho was also a frontier town, and this tax would have been collected there as well. The religious authorities also levied taxes on the people: (1) the temple tax of 1/2 shekel per person per year (Josephus refers to this tax several times; see, for example, *Antiquities* 16:28-30); (2) a tithe for the local synagogue; (3) and a poor tax (money collected for the needy; see Luke 21:1-4; 1 Corinthians 16:1-3).

3. The Galilean Ministry

1. John 3:24 states, "John, of course, had not yet been thrown into prison."

2. Tabgha is an Arabic corruption of the Greek *Heptapegon*, which means the "place of the seven springs." During the first century this area was known as Dalamanutha (see Mark 8:10). The springs of Tabgha have always been important to the fishing trade at the Sea of Galilee. For centuries the warm mineral water has drawn schools of fish to these coves in the winter months for centuries. Thus these would have been popular winter fishing waters for the fishermen of Capernaum in the first century.

3. Mendel Nun, one of Israel's leading authorities on fishing and the Sea of Galilee, writes: "Let us, at the start, state that fishing methods on the lake did not change from the time of the Second Temple up to modern times" (Mendel Nun, *The Sea of Galilee and Its Fishermen in the New Testament* [Tiberias, Israel: En Gev Press 1989], 5).

4. Josephus writes, "Accordingly he [John] was sent a prisoner, out of Herod's suspicious temper, to Macherus, the castle I before mentioned, and was there put to death" (*Antiquities* 18:119).

5. In Eastern thought, the answer to the question "What is God like?" is "God is like what God has done." We know what God has done because we have a record (Bible, Qu'ran). In this exchange, this perception is demonstrated by Jesus' saying to the followers of John, "Go and tell John what is happening." Jesus' response speaks to expectations expressed in Isaiah 61:1ff., which happens to be the passage quoted by Jesus in his announcement in Nazareth (see Luke 4:18-19).

6. Traditionally the church has thought of Jesus' ministry as lasting approximately three years. This figure has been based on an erroneous reading of the Gospel of John, which places Jesus in Jerusalem during festivals that might happen over a three-year period. The Synoptic Gospels imply a much shorter period of time for his ministry, and today scholars in Israel generally agree that the ministry of Jesus could not have lasted longer than one year.

7. John's Gospel does not report the arrest of the Baptist. Therefore, we cannot know exactly when this time of preparation ended and Jesus' ministry actually began. All we can say for certain is that, according to Mark's Gospel, Jesus' ministry began with the arrest of John the Baptist.

8. Today tourists who visit Israel are not able to visit the biblical site of Cana. The site where this miracle is reported to have occurred was known as Garis in the first century CE. An interesting theory tries to explain how this site came to be called Cana. It is suggested that when Queen Helena, the mother of Constantine, the first Christian emperor of the Roman Empire, made her pilgrimage to the Holy Land she asked to be taken to Cana. At that time no one was sure where the site was located. While the entourage moved northeast of Nazareth on their way to Tiberias, one of Helena's guides pointed out a place a few kilometers from Nazareth as biblical Cana. It seems he did not want to disappoint the queen. From that time, this site has been known as Cana. The actual site of biblical Cana was identified several years back and is not found near any road; reaching the site requires a considerable hike over rugged terrain.

9. In Matthew 13:55, we have a listing of the names of the brothers of Jesus. They are James, Joseph, Simon, and Judas. We are also told here that Jesus had sisters, but we are not told how many or their names.

10. Safrai and Stern, *The Jewish People in the First Century*, 2:829-30.

11. E. P. Sanders, *Judaism: Practice and Belief, 63 BCE-66 CE* (Philadelphia: Trinity Press International, 1992), 224.

12. In Mark 3 we read: "Then he went home (to Capernaum); and the crowd came together again, so that they could not even eat. When his family heard it, they went out to restrain him, for people were saying, 'He has gone out of his mind'" (Mark 3:19-21). "Then his mother and his brothers came; and standing outside they sent to him and called him. The crowd was sitting around him; and they said to him, 'Your mother and your brothers and sisters are outside, asking for you.' And he replied, 'Who are my mother and my brothers?' And looking at those who sat around him, he said, 'Here are my mother and brothers! Whoever does the will of God is my brother and sister, and mother'" (Mark 3:31-35).

The people of Nazareth followed the solar calendar, and the people of Capernaum, more contemporary and liberal, followed the lunar calendar. This understanding helps to clarify an encounter between Jesus and his brothers in John 7. Here the brothers of Jesus come to him and ask him to go with them to Jerusalem for the celebration of the Feast of Tabernacles. Jesus declines because, "My time has not yet come" (John 7:6). This is another example of Jesus' brothers' attempting to bring him back to their own theological position. Jesus informs his brothers that he no longer believes as they do, and he later goes to Jerusalem with his new "family," his disciples, a few days later and observes the Feast of Tabernacles based on the lunar calendar.

13. Bedouin are the nomadic people found throughout the Middle East. They are primarily shepherds and live in defined tribal areas.

14. David Flusser, *Jewish Sources in Early Christianity* (Tel Aviv: Mod Books, 1989), 22-23.

15. In Luke 13:10-17, we find the story of the healing of a woman who had been ill for some eighteen years. Jesus healed this woman on the sabbath and was condemned by the "leader of the synagogue" (v. 14). Jesus rebuts this condemnation by stating a classic Hillelian argument, and the leader of the synagogue is put to shame. Furthermore, the people respond positively to Jesus' act and to his reply to the Shammai criticism.

16. The word *Eremos* means, literally, "the quiet place" or the "lonely place."

When we read the words "quiet place" or "lonely place," as applied to Jesus' location, we should think that he is probably at the Eremos.

17. Matthew reports the healing of this leper following the Sermon on the Mount, but both Matthew and Mark locate this healing in the area of the Eermos.

18. Surrounding the courtyard of the insula would be a thatched eave about one meter in length. This would provide shade for people sitting on an interior bench, which would be found in the courtyard. This was a place for sitting with guests and neighbors to chat and also where Jesus would have taught when he met with the general populace in a house rather than the synagogue.

19. Fishermen in the first century would fish in waters near to their own villages. There are approximately forty fishing coves around the Sea of Galilee, and these can easily be divided among the villages, towns, and cities that surrounded the lake. See the map below:

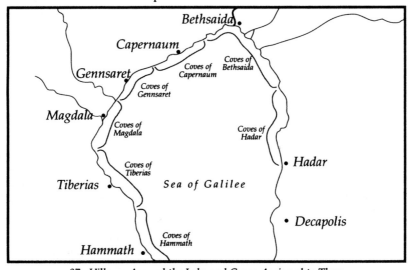

87. Villages Around the Lake and Coves Assigned to Them

20. Safrai and Stern, *The Jewish People of the First Century*, 2:828-29.

21. Herbert Danby, trans., *The Mishnah* (London: Oxford University Press, 1987), 148.

22. The Gospels refer to this place as the country of the Gadarenes (Matt. 8:28-34); the country of the Gerasenes (Mark 5:1-20; Luke 8:26-33). If the miracle did, in fact, take place in the area of what is known today as Kursi, this is nowhere near the biblical Gadara (located near Hammat Gader) or Geresa (located near Jerash in central Jordan). How the Gospel writers came to apply these names to this site is unknown.

23. The traditional location of the miracle of the healing of the demoniac is known today as Kursi. In the fifth century CE, a monastery was built there to commemorate this miracle of Jesus' healing. However, this is only a traditional site, and we have no knowledge of where, or whether, this encounter took place. By their stopping in this place, we see that Jesus and the disciples

are about to violate the laws of purity by traveling to a Gentile country and also by stepping onto land that is used as a cemetery.

24. Donin, *To Be a Jew*, 156. Rabbi Donin goes on to say:

> The *tallit*, a four-cornered robe with the required *tzitzit*, has thus become the garment traditionally worn by men during morning prayer services. In English, it is commonly called a "prayer shawl."

Before wrapping the tallit around oneself, it is held in both hands while standing, and the following blessing is recited: " . . . Blessed art Thou, Lord our God, King of the universe who has sanctified us with His commandments and commanded us to wrap ourselves in the *tzitzit*." The fringes (*tzitzit*) on the four corners of the *tallit* provide it with its religious significance.

Safrai says this concerning the *tallit* and *tzitzit*:

> Jesus dressed like the rest of the Hellenistic world, with a tunic and cloak (*talit*) above the underwear. The tunic was usually of linen and the cloak of wool, though the latter could also be of linen. Only a woven mixture of wool and linen was prohibited. Fringes . . . were attached to the four corners of a rectangular cloak, though not to one round in shape like the Roman toga; they were actually tassels, because each set of strings had to be folded and knotted, making a total of eight tassels. One of these was the "thread of blue," dyed with the blood of a snail found on the northern part of the coast. This "thread of blue" gradually disappeared since the dyeing process was expensive and the dye itself rare. (Safrai and Stern, *The Jewish People in the First Century*, 2:797)

25. It is likely that soldiers gambled for Jesus' *tallit* at the foot of the cross. Typically men wore four garments in the first century: an outer garment, an under garment, a turban or headdress, and sandals. A religious person might also wear a prayer shawl with valuable blue threads that could sold for potentially large sums of money. It is unlikely that soldiers would gamble for the old and worn garments of a peasant, but highly likely that they would cast lots for a valuable prayer shawl.

26. Some biblical references for each of these acts of hospitality are: (1) a drink of water, Matt. 10:42; John 4:7ff.; Rev. 22:17; (2) washing feet, Gen. 18:4; 19:2; Judg. 19:21; Luke 7:36ff.; John 13:4-11; 1 Tim. 5:10; (3) greeting with a kiss, Matt. 26:48-49; Mark 14:45; Luke 22:47; Rom. 16:16; 1 Cor. 16:20; (4) anointing or washing the head, Matt. 26:6-13; John 11:2; (5) offering something to eat, Matt. 26:23; Mark 14:20; John 13:26.

27. Hospitality was important in cultures throughout the Middle East in the first century CE, and it is still vital in the Middle East today. The laws of hospitality were so important in biblical times that Lot was willing to give up his virgin daughters to protect strangers in his house (Gen. 19:1-11). Deuteronomy 23:3-4 is another interesting passage: "No Ammorite or Moabite shall enter the assembly of the Lord; even to the tenth generation none belonging to them shall enter the assembly of the Lord forever; because they did not meet you with bread and with water on the way, when you came forth out of Egypt." The Israelites were forbidden to have any interaction with the Ammorites or Moabites, because these two groups did not show hospitality when the Israelites were wandering in the wilderness on their way to the Promised Land.

28. Other places where the Eremos is mentioned in the Gospels are Matthew 14:13, 15; Mark 1:35; 6:31-32, 35; Luke 4:42; 5:16; 9:12

29. Christian tradition locates the site of the first multiplication of the fish and loaves at Tabgha, located between biblical Capernaum and Gennesaret.

30. In winter and spring sudden storms on the Sea of Galilee are not unusual. The Sea of Galilee is almost 700 feet below sea level. Cool air from the Golan Heights meets the warm air coming off the lake, and these contribute to the sudden and unpredictable storms. Furthermore, in the springtime a strong wind known colloquially as the "sharkieh" comes off the Golan. The kind of storm reported in Mark 6 is common for this area, and it is probable that this storm, if an historical event, happened in the spring.

31. It is possible that in referring to this woman as a dog, the Gospel writers were aware of the practice in first-century Palestine of regarding all Gentiles as dogs. This reference is not directed specifically at this poor woman.

32. These seven nations are mentioned by name in Deuteronomy 7:1: "When the LORD your God brings you into the land that you are about to enter and occupy, and he clears away many nations before you—the Hittites, the Girgashites, the Amorites, the Canaanites, the Perizzites, the Hivites, and the Jebusites, seven nations mightier and more numerous than you."

33. The Gospel of Matthew reports: "Then he began to reproach the cities in which most of his mighty deeds had been done, because they did not repent." We are told that these cities, or villages, are Chorazin, Bethsaida, and Capernaum. It is quite amazing and ironic that so little of Jesus' ministry in Chorazin and Bethsaida are reported. The passage here in Mark 8 is the only explicit reference to a healing in Bethsaida. None are reported in Chorazin.

34. The three sources for the Jordan River are the Hermon Springs, found at Caesarea Philippi, the Dan River, and the Has Bani River in Lebanon.

35. See Charles R. Page II and Carl A. Volz, *The Land and the Book: An Introduction to the World of the Bible* (Nashville: Abingdon Press, 1993), 108.

36. Among additional references to the custom of the social contract of friendship for the giving and receiving of water are Matthew 10:40-42; Mark 9:38-41; and Revelation 22:17.

37. Often when I am in the Land, I ask persons I meet whether it is common for a son to make such a request of his father. Every response is no, that it would dishonor both the father and the son. This response conforms to a passage from the Torah.

"If someone has a stubborn and rebellious son who will not obey his father and mother, who does not heed them when they discipline him, then his father and his mother shall take hold of him and bring him out to the elders of his town at the gate of that place. They shall say to the elders of his town, 'This son of ours is stubborn and rebellious. He will not obey us. He is a glutton and a drunkard.' Then all the men of the town shall stone him to death. So you shall purge the evil from you midst; and all Israel will hear, and be afraid" (Deuteronomy 21:18-21).

Kenneth Bailey reports similar experiences: "For over fifteen years I have been asking people of all walks of life from Morocco to India and from Turkey to the Sudan about the implication's of a son's request for his inheritance while the father is still living. The answer has almost always been emphatically the same" (Kenneth E. Bailey, *Poet and Peasant and Through Peasant Eyes* [Grand Rapids: Eerdmans, 1983], 161-62).

38. Danby, *The Mishnah*, 377-78. The Torah provides that the firstborn son shall receive a double portion of the father's property as an inheritance. Therefore, the younger son in the parable received one-third of the father's property. (See Deut. 21:15-17.)

39. For those hearing the story, a "far country" would be the Decapolis. "Far away" does not mean far away in distance, but in custom. Thus the Gentiles were "far away from us" in custom and ethnicity.

40. Herding swine would have been repugnant to Jewish people in the first century. Thus this reference connotes that the younger had sunk to the lowest depths possible.

41. Bailey, *Poet and Peasant and Through Peasant Eyes*, 94.

42. For a good discussion of meals related to the ministry of Jesus, see Robert C. Morgan, *Who's Coming to Dinner? Jesus Made Known in the Breaking of Bread* (Nashville: Abingdon Press, 1992).

4. The Judean Ministry

1. Jesus was familiar with the Wadi Qelt from his Wilderness experience. The Wadi Qelt is a shortcut to Jerusalem from Jericho and the Jordan Valley, and it would allow him to travel to Jerusalem without as much attention as he might have encountered on the main highway.

2. David Flusser, *Jewish Sources in Early Christianity* (Tel Aviv: Mod Books, 1989), 23-24.

3. Herbert Danby, trans., *The Mishnah* (London: Oxford University Press, 1987), 500, note 11. Bethphage is also mentioned as the city limits in Mishnah Menahoth 11:2.

4. Josephus also discusses Solomon's rise to the throne and the king's processional with the king riding on a donkey in *Antiquities of the Jews* 7:351ff.

5. Even today the image of the palm branch can be seen on some Israeli currency.

6. The Romans occupied Palestine with a superior, better equipped, well-staffed, and well-trained army. They were the best fighting machine in the world at the time. Only a miracle could help the Jewish people to regain their independence. The conditions in Palestine during the Roman Period were similar to the Palestine of Antiochus IV. The people witnessed a miracle during the Maccabean Revolt and perhaps another would happen at this time.

7. This church was built in 1954–55 in the form of a teardrop to commemorate Jesus' weeping over the city.

8. It is obvious that this centurion was a sympathizer or convert to the Jewish faith. "He loves our nation, and built us our synagogue" (Luke 7:5).

9. Ellis Rivkin, *What Crucified Jesus? The Political Execution of a Charismatic* (Nashville: Abingdon Press, 1984), 22-23.

10. Ibid., 23.

11. Josephus *Antiquities of the Jews* 13:298.

12. Rivkin, *What Crucified Jesus?* 31-33.

13. Jesus' encounter with the teachers at the Temple, reported in Luke 2:41-49, would have taken place in this colonnade.

14. On the Shema, Donin remarks: "Every Jew is required to recite the Bibli-

cal passage known as the Shema (Hear O Israel) twice a day, morning and evening, in fulfillment of the precept: 'And you shall talk of them. . . . When you lie down and when you rise up.' The morning and evening prayer service incorporate the passage. Even though the Shema is an integral part of the morning and evening services, the Shema is not, technically speaking, a prayer. It is a declaration of faith. It is an affirmation of the unity of God that reminds us of our obligations to Him." (*To Be a Jew: A Guide to Jewish Observance in Contemporary Life* [New York: Basic Books, 1972], 163-64). See also Mishnah Berakoth 1-3.

15. The gates at the southern end of the Temple Mount were known as the Eastern and Western Huldah Gates, named after the prophetess Huldah (see 2 Chron. 34:22-28). These gates were the primary entrance into and exit from the Temple for the priests, but others could use them as well. The eastern gates were used as the entrance, and the western gates were the exit. However, if a person was in mourning they would enter the Temple through the exit and exit through the entrance, then people would know they were grieving and could offer consolation.

16. This might seem like a contradiction, considering that Jesus had attached himself to the House of Hillel. However, when we consider that the time frame for his move from Nazareth to Capernaum and on to Jerusalem was short and that his initial optimism regarding the Pharisees' potential for reaching the people had been misplaced, we see that his response is not so surprising. Jesus had aligned himself with the Pharisees (House of Hillel) because he believed that they would make a difference in people's lives. Yet, the goal of the Pharisees was the same as that for any other organization: institutional preservation. Ultimately, their goal was not to reach the people but to preserve the status quo. Jesus expected more from them, but they did not produce. His reaction was simply to pour out his soul on these steps, which constituted a break from the House of Hillel. We always criticize the ones to whom we are the closest. This is human nature. This is another situation when the humanity of Jesus is most apparent. Jesus expected more from the Pharisees, in general, and the House of Hillel, more particularly. After they had failed to respond to the needs of the general public, he broke with them and verbally attacked them, as he had physically attacked the money changers and Sadducees on Monday.

17. This is the most important of Jewish cemeteries in the Holy Land. Jewish tradition suggests that when the Messiah comes, those buried on the Mount of Olives will be the first to rise in the general resurrection. Jewish people have been buried here since the time of King David. Today, Israel's most prominent leaders and the very wealthy are buried here.

18. Think of examples today of how easily people are swayed by public opinion, the manipulation of the media, to turn on individuals. Human nature is human nature, whether we are talking about the first century or the twentieth. The masses still love a lynching.

19. Even today, particularly among, but not limited to, the Bedouin, men do not carry water. This is considered "women's work."

20. The central headquarters for the Essenes was Qumran. However, Qumran was destroyed by an earthquake in 31 BCE, and the Essenes established a new headquarters in the Upper City of Jerusalem. Perhaps Herod the Great gave them a place for their monastery, for they returned to Qumran only after

Herod's death. Jerusalem remained the central headquarters for the Essenes from 31 to 4 BCE.

Josephus informs us that Herod had a special fondness for the Essenes because when he was a young boy a member of the Essenes prophesied that Herod would one day be king of the Jews:

> Now there was one of the Essenes, whose name was Manahem, who had this testimony, that he not only conducted his life after an excellent manner, but had the foreknowledge of future events given him by God also. This man once saw Herod when he was a child, and going to school, and saluted him as king of the Jews; but he, thinking that either he did not know him, or that he was in jest, put him in mind that he was but a private man; but Manahem smiled to himself, and clapped his backside with his hand, and said, "However that be, thou wilt be king, and wilt begin thy reign happily, for God finds thee worthy of it; and do thou remember the blows that Manahem hath given thee, as being a signal of the change of thy fortune.". . . Now at the time Herod did not attend to what Manahem said, as having no hopes of such advancement; but a little afterward; when he was so fortunate as to be advanced to the dignity of king, and was in the height of his dominion, he sent for Manahem . . . and from that time he continued to honor all the Essenes. (Josephus *Antiquities of the Jews* 15:373-378)

21. A *triclinium* table would have been a three-sided, U-shaped table at which persons would recline to eat their meals. People would have reclined on their left elbow (or propped themselves against the table on the left side of their bodies) and eaten with their right hand.

In Near Eastern society, it is forbidden to eat with the left hand. The left hand is considered unclean because it was used for personal hygiene. The Bible speaks to this in Ecclesiastes 10:2: "The heart of the wise inclines to the right, but the heart of a fool to the left." The New Testament also picks up this idea: "When the Son of Man comes in his glory, and all the angels with him, then he will sit on the throne of his glory. All the nations will be gathered before him, and he will separate people one from another as a shepherd separates the sheep from the goats, and he will put the sheep at his right hand and the goats at the left" (Matt. 25:31-33).

22. This arrangement is suggested in a teaching of Jesus found in Luke 14:7-11: "When he noticed how the guests chose the places of honor, he told them a parable. 'When you are invited by someone to a wedding banquet, do not sit down at the place of honor, in case someone more distinguished than you has been invited by your host; and the host who invited both of you may come and say to you, "Give this person your place," and then in disgrace you would start to take the lowest place. But when you are invited, go and sit down at the lowest place, so that when your host comes, he may say to you, "Friend, move up higher"; then you will be honored in the presence of all who sit at the table with you. For all who exalt themselves will be humbled, and those who humble themselves will be exalted.' "

23. Robert C. Morgan, *Who's Coming to Dinner? Jesus Made Known in the Breaking of Bread* (Nashville: Abingdon Press, 1992), 129.

24. There has been much speculation about the identity of this disciple. Some have thought that this person was the disciple John. Others argue that it is not. In Israel it is generally assumed that this person is indeed John, and I have no argument with this identification. For our purposes here, we will assume this is John.

25. The offering of the sop is an ancient Middle Eastern custom, a gift of hospitality offered to a visitor who was considered to be the guest of honor. The sop is offered when the host takes bread, breaks it, and then dips it in a salad or sauce (like humus), and then offers it to one of his guests. The first recipient of the sop is always the guest of honor.

John indicates that Judas is the recipient of the sop and, thus, is seated in position three John wants to underscore, as ironic as it might seem, that Judas is the guest of honor at the Last Supper.

26. The word *Gethsemane* means, literally, "olive press." In the Synoptic Gospels Jesus is both literally and metaphorically in the "olive press" being pressed out in agony.

27. The Basilica of the Agony, also known colloquially as the Church of All Nations, is built over the ruins of earlier churches built on the site during the Byzantine and Crusader Periods. The present-day church was built in 1924. Funding for the church came from countries throughout the world. This is how the church has come to be known as the Church of All Nations.

28. According to Safrai and Stern, the man referred to as Annas was actually named Ananus, who was deposed by Valerius Gratus, the last governor to serve Judea under Augustus. The high priest called Caiaphas in the New Testament was actually named Joseph Caiaphas. Stern writes:

> Valerius Gratus deposed Ananus from the high priesthood and appointed Ishmael ben Phiabi, a member of an Egyptian Jewish family which had risen to prominence in Herod's reign; then after a brief period again appointed one of Ananus' family, Eleazar son of Ananus. Eleazar served in the high priesthood no more than a year and was replaced by Simeon son of Camith. After a short time Gratus appointed Joseph Caiaphas, who was, with Ananus, the most important high priest in the period of the first governors and served longer than any other incumbent in the procuratorial period. The Gospel of John makes it clear that he was the son-in-law of Ananus and the two collaborated to determine the policy of the high priesthood. (Shemuel Safrai and Menahem Stern, eds., *The Jewish People in the First Century*, 2 vols. (Assen: Van Gorcum; Philadelphia: Fortress Press, 1974–76), 1:349)

29. Ibid., 2:600.

30. Today the ruins of the traditional house of Caiaphas are found beneath the Church of St. Peter in Gallicantu, or St. Peter at the Crowing of the Cock, near present-day Mt. Zion. However, this site is only a tradition; nothing exists to support the claim. The church is named for Peter's denial of Jesus three times before the crowing of the cock, as Jesus had predicted.

31. There was a custom in the ancient world that if a person ate a meal with a "sinner," the persons would never again be allowed to testify in open court. Is it possible that Jesus' silence was based on his willingness to eat with people like Levi and Zacchaeus? People were more important to Jesus than were archaic regulations.

32. Rivkin, *What Crucified Jesus?* 34-36.

33. Hendrikus Boers, *Who Was Jesus? The Historical Jesus and the Synoptic Gospels* (New York: Harper & Row, 1989), 67-69.

34. Josephus *Antiquities of the Jews* 18:55ff.

35. Ibid., 18:60ff.

36. See Safrai and Stern, *The Jewish People in the First Century*, 2:320.

37. For a detailed account of all of the various violations that would have led to scourging, see Mishnah Makkoth 3:1ff.

38. Charles R. Page II and Carl A. Volz, *The Land and the Book: An Introduction to the World of the Bible* (Nashville: Abingdon Press, 1993), 198. This event is also reported in John 19:1-4.

39. Herod Agrippa ordered the construction of a "third" to the north of the city in roughly 40–41 CE, which brought the quarry into the city. Since under Jewish Law a cemetery would not be permitted within the walls of a city, the quarry ceased to be used as a cemetery at this time. Before this time, however, the quarry and its cemetery were located outside the city walls.

40. Two of these tombs are the Tomb of the Kings, just north of the Albright Institute, and the Sanhedrin Tombs to the northwest of the city.

41. See Page and Volz, *The Land and the Book,* 195.

42. Two very interesting traditions are associated with the execution and resurrection site of Jesus. An early Byzantine Church tradition contends that Jesus was executed over the burial place of Adam, our primeval father, and that the blood from Jesus' wounds washed over the skull of Adam, washing away the pollution of original sin. Consequently, the place came to be known in Christian tradition as the "place of the skull," or Golgotha. The tradition also attests that Jesus was buried in a new tomb located in a garden. Our primeval ancestors are said to have fallen from God's grace into sin in a garden, the Garden of Eden. Because of the atonement activity of God and Jesus, humanity has been restored to grace in a garden.

It is quite possible that both of these, the place of the skull and the garden, are metaphors, symbols of theological importance in the primitive church that found their way into the New Testament. Humanity fell from grace in a garden and was restored in a garden. Jesus was executed at the place of the skull. In fact, however, we have no idea what this execution site was called in the first century CE, but it is improbable that it was "Golgotha." A contemporary mosaic of Jesus' execution and burial memorializes this Byzantine tradition.

43. See Josephus *The Jewish Wars* 7:203 and 5:449ff., where Josephus discusses Roman crucifixions in relationship to the First Jewish Revolt.

44. Safrai and Stern, *The Jewish People in the First Century,* 2:776-77.

45. The Mishnah offers a description of the size and dimensions of a typical tomb that is consistent with first-century tombs found in present-day Jerusalem:

> If a man sold to his fellow a place in which to make a tomb (so, too, if a man received from his fellow a place in which to make him a tomb), he must make the inside of the vault four cubits by six, and open within it eight niches, three on this side, three on that side, and two opposite (the doorway). The niches must be four cubits long, seven handbreadths high, and six wide. R. Simeon says: He must make the inside of the vault four cubits by eight and open up within it thirteen niches, four on this side, four on that side, three opposite (the doorway) and one to the right of the doorway and one to the left. He must make a courtyard at the opening of the vault, six cubits by six, space enough for the bier and its bearers; and he may open up within it two other vaults, one on either side. R. Simeon says: Four, one on each of its four sides. Rabban Simeon b. Gamaliel says: All depends on the nature of the rock. (Mishnah Baba Bathra 6:8; see Danby, *The Mishnah,* 375).

46. *Kokhim* were burial niches where a body would be interred until it had decomposed. Following decomposition, the bones would be collected and kept in a stone box, known as an ossuary. The size of the ossuary would depend on the size of the deceased's longest bone. Following the collection of the bones, the ossuary would be placed somewhere in the tomb complex or perhaps buried in the ground. *Arcosolia* were larger niches where a body could be interred in a casket.

47. Safrai and Stern, *The Jewish People in the First Century*, 2:781-82.

48. Bargil Pixner, a Benedictine archaeologist assigned to the Dormition Abbey and to Tabgha, and who is also an adjunct faculty member of the Jerusalem Center, has stated in various lectures over the years that Luke has a very poor sense of the geography of Galilee. However, Luke has a very accurate knowledge of the geography of Judea and Jerusalem. Pixner theorizes that this is because Luke had an urban background and possibly wrote from Jerusalem. Perhaps this helps to explain the sudden shift from Galilee to Judea.

49. Page and Volz, *The Land and the Book*, 181-82.

50. Some of the ancient manuscripts of the New Testament contain the following verse, inserted at verse 4: "For an angel of the Lord went down in certain seasons into the pool, and troubled the water; whoever stepped in first after the troubling of the water was healed of whatever he had."

51. The god Serapis was produced as a result of the synthesis of the Egyptian gods Osiris and Apis, and dates from the time of Ptolemy I, in roughly 300 BCE.

52. Joachim Jeremias, *Jerusalem in the Time of Jesus* (Philadelphia: Fortress Press, 1969), 303. The four lists of despised trades listed by Jeremias are taken from Mishnah Kiddushin, Mishnah Ketuboth, the Babylonian Talmud Kiddushin, and the Babylonian Talmud Sanhedrin. Some of the despised trades listed include ass driver, camel driver, shepherd (or herdsman), physician, butcher, dung collector, tanner, barber, gambler, usurer, and, of course, tax collector.

SELECTED BIBLIOGRAPHY

General

Aharoni, Yohanan. *The Land of the Bible: A Historical Geography*. Philadelphia: Westminster Press, 1979.

Beasley, James R., et al. *An Introduction to the Bible*. Nashville: Abingdon Press, 1991.

Boers, Hendrikus. *Who Was Jesus? The Historical Jesus and the Synoptic Gospels*. San Francisco: Harper & Row, 1989.

Cartlidge, David R., and David L. Dungan. *Documents for the Study of the Gospels*. Philadelphia: Fortress Press, 1980.

Flusser, David. *Jewish Sources in Early Christianity*. Tel Aviv: Mod Books, 1989.

——— . *The Spiritual History of the Dead Sea Sect*. Tel Aviv: Mod Books, 1989.

Knibb, Michael A. *The Qumran Community*. New York: Cambridge University Press, 1988.

Morgan, Robert C. *Who's Coming to Dinner? Jesus Made Known in the Breaking of Bread*. Nashville: Abingdon Press, 1991.

Nun, Mendal. *The Sea of Galilee and Its Fishermen in the New Testament*. Kibbutz Ein Gev: Kinnereth, 1989.

Patterson, Stephen J. *The Gospel of Thomas and Jesus*. Sonoma, Calif.: Polebridge Press, 1993.

Rivkin, Ellis. *What Crucified Jesus? The Political Execution of a Charismatic*. Nashville: Abingdon Press, 1984.

Sanders, E. P., and Margaret Davies. *Studying the Synoptic Gospels*. London: SCM Press, 1991.

Archaeology/Anthropology

Aharoni, Yohanan. *The Archaeology of the Land of Israel*. Philadelphia: Westminster Press, 1982.

Bailey, Kenneth E. *Poet and Peasant, and Through Peasant Eyes*. Grand Rapids: Eerdmans, 1983.

Batey, Richard A. *Jesus and the Forgotten City*. Grand Rapids: Baker Book House, 1991.

Ben-Dov, Meir. *In the Shadow of the Temple*. Jerusalem: Keter Publishing House, 1982.

Connolly, Peter. *Living in the Time of Jesus of Nazareth*. Jerusalem: Steimatzky, 1992.

Finegan, Jack. *Myth and Mystery: An Introduction to the Pagan Religions of the Biblical World*. Grand Rapids: Baker Book House, 1989.

Matthews, Victor H. *Manners and Customs in the Bible*. Peabody, Mass.: Hendrickson Publishers, 1988.

McRay, John. *Archaeology and the New Testament*. Grand Rapids: Baker Book House, 1991.

Murphy-O'Connor, Jerome. *The Holy Land: An Archaeological Guide from Earliest Times to 1700*. 3rd ed. Oxford: Oxford University Press, 1992.

Page, Charles R., II, and Carl A. Volz. *The Land and the Book: An Introduction to the World of the Bible*. Nashville: Abingdon Press, 1993.

Schoville, Keith N. *Biblical Archaeology in Focus*. Grand Rapids: Baker Book House, 1986.

Stambaugh, John E., and David L. Balch. *The New Testament in Its Social Environment*. Philadelphia: Westminster, 1986.

Biblical History

Bickerman, Elias J. *The Jews in the Greek Age*. Cambridge, Mass.: Harvard University Press, 1988.

Charlesworth, James H. *Jesus and the Dead Sea Scrolls*. New York: Doubleday, 1992.

Eusebius. *The Ecclesiastical History*. Translated by Christian Frederick Cruse. Grand Rapids: Baker Book House, 1987.

Horsley, Richard A., and John S. Hanson. *Bandits, Prophets, and Messiahs*. San Francisco: Harper & Row, 1985.

Jeremias, Joachim. *Jerusalem in the Time of Jesus*. Philadelphia: Fortress Press, 1969.

Josephus. *The Works of Josephus Complete and Unabridged*. Translated by William Whiston. Peabody, Mass.: Hendrickson Publishers, 1987.

Pritz, Ray A. *Nazarene Jewish Christianity*. Jerusalem: Maganes Press of the Hebrew University, 1992.

Rivkin, Ellis. *A Hidden Revolution*. Nashville: Abingdon Press, 1978.

Roth, Cecil. *A History of the Jews: From Earliest Times Through the Six Day War*. New York: Schocken Books, 1970.

Safrai, Shemuel, and Menahem Stern. *The Jewish People of the First Century*. Volumes 1 and 2. Assen: Van Gorcum; Philadelphia: Fortress Press, 1974–76.

Hellenistic/Roman History

Grant, Michael. *History of Rome*. New York: Macmillan, 1978.

Kagan, Donald. *Botsford and Robinson's Hellenistic History*. New York: Macmillan, 1969.

Roebuck, Carl. *The World of Ancient Times*. New York: Charles Scribner's Sons, 1966.

Sinnigen, William G., and Charles Alexander Robinson, Jr. *Ancient History from Prehistoric Times to the Death of Justinian*. New York: Macmillan, 1981.

Sinnigen, William G., and Arthur E. R. Boak. *A History of Ancient Rome to AD 565*. New York: Macmillan, 1977.

Jewish Life and Faith

Charlesworth, James H. *Jesus Within Judaism*. New York: Doubleday, 1988.

Donin, Hayim Halevy. *To Be a Jew: A Guide to Jewish Observance in Contemporary Life*. New York: Basic Books, 1972.

Lipman, Eugene J. *The Mishnah: Oral Traditions of Judaism*. New York: Schocken Books, 1976.

The Mishnah. Translated by Herbert Danby. Oxford: Oxford University Press, 1987.

Neusner, Jacob. *Invitation to the Talmud*. San Francisco: Harper & Row, 1984.

Sanders, E. P. *Jewish Law from Jesus to the Mishnah*. Philadelphia: Trinity Press International, 1990.

———— . *Judaism Practice and Belief 63 BCE–66 CE*. Philadelphia: Trinity Press International, 1992.

Steinsaltz, Adin. *The Essential Talmud*. New York: Basic Books, 1976.

Zeitland, Irving M. *Jesus and the Judaism of His Time*. New York: Polity Press, 1988.

SCRIPTURE INDEX

SUBJECT INDEX

CPSIA information can be obtained at www.ICGtesting.com
Printed in the USA
BVOW012049171212

308472BV00005B/173/P